GEEKS BEARING GIFTS
How the Computer World Got This Way

Ted Nelson

Mindful Press, 2008

GEEKS BEARING GIFTS

COVER. Why is Bill smiling so charmingly while in police custody? Because he knows it's no big deal, and his future looks as bright as he is.

Public-domain photograph by Albuquerque police department.

See discussion of rights issues for this picture in Chapter -18.

Geeks Bearing Gifts Edition 1.0

©2008 Theodor Holm Nelson. All rights reserved.

MINDFUL PRESS, distributed by Lulu.com.

ISBN: 978-0-578-00438-9

TRADEMARKS. All trademarks are those of their respective rightsholders. Let us note in particular the trademark UNIX® and get it over with. The current rightsholder as of this week is the Open Group (rights to the Unix trademark have passed around the field like a bad penny). They want "UNIX" to be in all-capital letters, but that gets obnoxious fast, particularly since it is mentioned here many times, so we have been sparing in the all-capitalization.

Other registered trademarks of particular concern include Adobe Acrobat®, Adobe Flash®, Adobe Photoshop®, Adobe PostScript®, GNU®, Linux®, Microsoft Windows®, Microsoft Word®, Microsoft Excel®, Xanadu®, ...

GEEKS BEARING GIFTS

"If you enjoy sausage or respect the law,
do not enquire as to how either is made."-- anon.

"War is too important to be left to the generals." --Georges Clemenceau

"There's more than one way to do it." -- Larry Wall

To Doug

He knew, and kept on

CONTENTS, negative chapter numbers first

PREFACE   1
INTRODUCTION   3

Chapter (-27) **Hierarchy** (ancient beginnings) 6
Chapter (-26) **Alphabets** (ancient beginnings) 10
Chapter (-25) **Punctuation** (ancient beginnings) 17
Chapter (-24) **Encryption** (ancient beginnings) 20
Chapter (-23) **Making Documents Hierarchical** (18th Century) 24
Chapter (-22) **They All Invented Computers** (1822) 26
Chapter (-21) **They All Idealized Computers** (1843) 30
Chapter (-20) **Database** (1884) 36
Chapter (-19) **Voting Machines** (1892) 39
Chapter (-18) **Intellectual property** (1923) 42
Chapter (-17) **The Mainframe Era** (1946) 49
Chapter (-16) **Computer Sound and Music** (1947) 52
Chapter (-15) **Computer Graphics in Two Dimensions** (1950) 54
Chapter (-14) **Computer Games** (1951) 59
Chapter (-13) **Disk Drive Wars** (1956) 62
Chapter (-12) **Engelbart's NLS** (1958) 68
Chapter (-11) **Xanadu** (1960) 71
Chapter (-10) **Computer Graphics in Three Dimensions** (1960) 76
Chapter (-9) **The ARPANET Gets the Message Across** (1962) 81
Chapter (-8) **Instant Messaging and Texting** (1960s) 87
Chapter (-7) **Computer Movies** (1963) 89
Chapter (-6) **Shared Texts** (1965) 93
Chapter (−5) **Email** (1965) 95
Chapter (-4) **Hypertext Goes Down A Wrong-Way Street** (1967) 98
Chapter (-3) **Object-Oriented Programming** (1967) 101
Chapter (-2) **Local Networking** (1970) 104
Chapter (-1) **Datapoint— the Personal Computer with a Mainframe Attitude** (1970) 106

GEEKS BEARING GIFTS

Chapter 0 UNIX— Modern Computer History Begins (1970) 108

Chapter 1 **Malware and Security** (1973) 116
Chapter 2 **The Era of Dinky Computers: Kits and Stunts** (1974) 120
Chapter 3 **The PUI Simplifies the Computer** (1974) 122
Chapter 4 **Paperdigm: Computer As Paper Simulator** (1974) 129
Chapter 5 **The PUI as Writer's Block** (1974) 132
Chapter 6 **Personal Computing** (1977) 135
Chapter 7 **The World Wars: Consumer Operating Systems** (1977) 136
Chapter 8 **Spreadsheet** (1979) 151
Chapter 9 **The Domain Name System** (1983) 153
Chapter 10 **Free Software, GNU, Open Source and Linux (Gnu/Linux)** (1983) 156
Chapter 11 **The World Wars Go Mobile** (1983) 159
Chapter 12 **The Internet— Enjoy It While You Can** (1989) 161
Chapter 13 **The Simple Early Web** (1989) 165
Chapter 14 **PUI on the Internet— the Web Browser Salad** (1992) 167
Chapter 15 **The URL Unifies Net Addresses** (1994) 170
Chapter 16 **Web Biz: The Dot-Com World and the New Monopolies** (1995) 172
Chapter 17 **Streaming Goes Private** (1995) 175
Chapter 18 **Google** (1996) 178
Chapter 19 **Cyberfashion** (1996) 180
Chapter 20 **Web 2.0— Community and Cattle Pen** (2004) 182

- - - - - -

Chapter 21 **The Myth of Computer Technology** 186
Chapter 22 **Why We Fight** 190

GEMS BEARING GIFTS

PREFACE (sources and thanks)

I had a huge amount of material when I sat down to put this book together but I didn't know half of this stuff. I started fact-checking and found wonderful new things that had to go in, and I still have a huge amount of material that isn't in here yet.

Helping me understand many of these intricacies for nearly two decades has been my good and knowing friend Andrew Pam. I have also gotten a number of clarifications from my good friends John R. Levine and Arthur Bullard.

I have learned a great deal from Dave Farber's excellent mailing list on technical politics, which I highly recommend (interesting-people.net). And the greatest bulk of information, surprising insights as well as facts, I have gotten at Wikipedia, which for all its faults (see Chapter 20) is darn good.

I must give special thanks, without further elucidation, to Yuzuru Tanaka, Kay Nishi, Hajime Ohiwa, Wendy Hall and Bill Dutton. Special thanks are due to all my special friends in Japan, England, France, Finland, Brazil and the USA.

Special thanks too to the Engelbarts—notably Doug, Ballard, Karen, and Christina-- for warmth, hospitality and understanding over the years.

Most of all love and thanks to my sweetpartner, Systems Angel and team-mate Marlene Mallicoat, for years of support, systems help, and wonderfulness.

> **MISSING CONTENT.** So much, and so many people, are left out that belong even in this short book. I have tons more material, but wanted to get this out in 2008. If You The Public want another edition, I'll try to put in a lot more.
>
> **NEW INFORMATION IN THIS BOOK, IF ANY**. To mark certain items that I got from people themselves, rather

than written sources, I am using the academic convention "personal communication" in footnotes. These, and Chapters -11 and -4, constitute the only new information in this book; anything else here that's not from written sources or general knowledge is my own interpretation.

IF YOU CAN LOOK SOMETHING UP EASILY, I don't bother to tell you exactly where but give you enough information followed by § ("section mark").

PICTURE SOURCES. Screenshots are from my own machine unless otherwise stated. Other uncredited pictures are public domain, mostly from Wikipedia. My own photographs are marked with furthermore. Photographs from can't-remember-where are marked with ¿.

QUOTATION MARKS. For exact quotations, when known, I use double quotation marks, for inexact quotes single quotes.

SPELLINGS.
    Spelling of "tekkie". I have used what Bertolt Brecht called the "hardened spelling."
    Spelling of "PARCie". This is a hard one. Perhaps more literate would be PARQie, but that goes off the deep end. "Parkie" would be the next best alternative.

CAPITALIZATION. Simply for convenience, I have skipped many of the up-and-down spellings of different company names and products. This is aesthetically right but morally wrong, and should be corrected in the next edition, if any.

INTRODUCTION

Summary. This book is a brief introduction to today's computer ideas and where they came from. Most of the basic methods were developed in the last fifty years, and mostly are all software, and are mostly understandable. But it's very hard to get an overview. That's what this book is meant to provide.

With an emphasis on disagreements and conflicts.

But laying out these subjects has been extremely difficult. I have ended up dividing computer history into some sixty topics, presented as short stories on particular topics which continue on into the present day.

This is highly condensed.

We are prisoners in a fantasy world built of incompatible pieces and broken dreams; and this is called "technology", so nobody questions it.

A tangle and cacophony of gadgets and programs confront us. This mess includes our personal computers, the narly menus in equipment we buy, our mobile phones, recorded answering systems we must deal with when we call companies, cameras and cars and music players.

Fundamentally these are hidden software, and many of the software ideas are comprehensible-- or were, once, to their creators. The problem is understanding the ideas first, then figuring out the !"£$% menus.

Most people don't know where the software ideas all came from, let alone what they are. In the briefest and most superficial way I will be telling you a little of both. And mainly this book is about the utter randomness of how it all came about.

Today's computer world makes no more sense than the layout of London or the U.S. Internal Revenue Code. These things can only be understood historically.

But histories of computers tend to be accounts of heroes trudging a straight upward path. In most cases this does violence to the truth. I want to make clear how varied and conflicting have been the initiatives of what we call computer technology. I want to show here the huge variety of alternatives and disagreements and accidental lines of causality. The myth of 'technology' (discussed more below) is a myth of unidirectional progress that leaves out the ideas, disagreements, maneuvers, forgotten possibilities and politics.

Everything cross-connects and criss-crosses. Everything influenced everything else, kind of. All these topics interpenetrate and overlap and continue today. Dividing it up into topics has been very difficult. There is no good sequence to tell these things.

I have ended up dividing computer history into some sixty topics. I had no such plan at the beginning, but it became increasingly necessary to break topics further and further apart. I am presenting them as very short stories on each the particular topic. Each story continues to the present day from some particular beginning in time; I have ordered the stories by those beginnings, as best I could estimate them, placing arbitrary thumbtacks in the river of time.

I have chosen UNIX as the pivot, since so much led into it and so much has resulted from it. As told here, everything led to Unix and everything has come from it. This is as good a simplification as any.

This is a summary of what "everyone knows", just hitting high points of history-- mostly the standard view; but pointing out more conflicts than are usually presented. 80% of this is well known, 10% is little-known interesting stuff I've found out, and 10% is my own point of view.

TN
December 2008

THE WAR STORIES

"War stories" is how computer people often refer to their personal anecdotes and project histories. (In the 1950s, "war stories" referred to the histories that veterans of World War II would swap when they got together. The term is not so much heard now.)

Chapter -27 Hierarchy (ancient beginnings)

Summary.   Hierarchy is the official metaphysic of the computer world. (Aristotle, the medieval Catholic Church and the Dewey Decimal System have all reinforced this concept,) Many tekkies think all structure is hierarchical, and have arranged not to see any other kinds.

They say if you have a hammer everything looks like a nail.   Today's hierarchical computer tools (especially object-oriented languages and XML) make hierarchy an imposition, not an option. Current tools cannot represent the tangles of the real world.

HIERARCHY IN RELIGION.   Religion has always placed gods above men, but in polytheism-- the gods of Greece, Rome, India and so on-- the gods tend to be celebrities with different powers, among whom you cam shop around for favors.

Monotheism may have been invented by the pharaoh Akhnaton. (Some, like James Breasted, consider Akhnaton to have been a great man; others, like Nicholas Reeves, think Akhnaton was using the one-god story to support his own centralized power. Some, like Immanuel Velikovsky, believe that monotheism went from Akhnaton to Moses, giving him the idea for the First Commandment— thus creating the monotheistic religions of the Middle East which are very much with us still). In any case, going to monotheism puts you in a tighter situation, with one alleged Being to please and placate. Having only that god to appeal to, and nobody else to turn to, makes obedience essential and thus strengthens a hierarchical picture of the world.

HIERARCHY IN PHILOSOPHY: mainly one guy.   The Greek philosopher Aristotle saw everything in terms of hierarchy. (Some say that the Catholic Church celebrated Aristotle because this supported their iron hierarchical position of central authority.)*

*Bernard Smith, personal communication.

HIERARCHY THROUGH THE AGES. The medieval Catholic Church consciously adopted the structure of the Roman army, and brought monasteries and nunneries to heel by requiring them to have the same structure-- one person in charge, reporting to Rome. Cynics say that obedience to this hierarchical chain was necessary in order to assure a steady stream of funds to the Vatican. (When its hierarchical authority was challenged by the Protestant Reformation, the power and income of the Roman church were greatly lessened.)

HIERARCHY AS COMPUTER RELIGION. A similarly religious view of the world as hierarchical is adopted widely within the technical community. Hierarchy is the official metaphysic of the computer world. Many tekkies think all structure is hierarchical, and have arranged not to see any other kinds.

Unix established a fully hierarchical filesystem in 1970.

In the 1960s an interesting hierarchical form of enumeration was created by computer guys, Backus-Naur form. Now that has grown to a world standardization of an absolutely hierarchical structure system, XML, which pretends to be neutral.

They say if you have a hammer everything looks like a nail. Today's hierarchical computer tools (especially object-oriented languages and XML) make hierarchy a mandatory imposition, not an option. Current tools cannot represent cross-connection, interpenetration, overlap, or the other tangles of the real world-- let alone opinions about it.

Hierarchical interfaces. The hierarchical mentality gives us interfaces with unnecessary steps. Having made your choice, you have to back out of it in several levels. EXAMPLE: having selected a new icon for a Windows shortcut, it takes two steps to affirm this. You have to accept the first OK, then the second, clearly only because the paradigm pointlessly requires it.

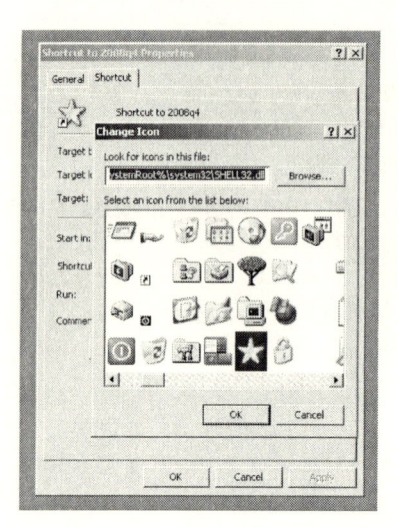

NONHIERARCHICAL STRUCTURES OF COMPUTERDOM.
There are a number of persistent data structures in the computer world which are not hierarchical, but they are marginalized. These include—
- .mbx format (basic for storing mail locally; overlap has to be handled by assigning a given email to multiple "mailboxes")
- relational database, storing structures as rows and columns.
- spreadsheet
- the web storage format at the Internet Archive, which concatenates pages consecutively with their addresses in large files
- hyperthogonal structure, an orthogonal irregular structure for generalized representation
- "mind map" structures of relationships
- the heap, for entities which arrive in arbitrary form

These structures are ways of capturing and representing what hierarchy cannot. However, none of these has the generalized leverage of the hierarchical tradition, and the psychological hold of hierarchy on the computer world seems unbreakable.

THE OVERALL PROBLEM.

Wanting to pull you into their paradigm, some people impose a structure they think is good for you and will clarify your thinking (no, it means you'll think like THEM.)

By forcing everything into hierarchy (which many think is the only kind of structure) it is impossible for many tekkies to perceive anything else, and they teach beginners that it's the necessary structure of computers, and the universe.

Today's hierarchical computer tools impose hierarchy where it may not exist; they can model the hierarchical aspects of the world but not the vital remainder.

Chapter -26 Alphabets (ancient beginnings)

Summary. Phonetic alphabets are only one form of writing, but they're the form that runs the computer world. Our alphabet derives from the Phoenician; upper case is introduced under Charlemagne in the 800s.

Then text is represented electrically-- in upper case because God was thought to require it. Three men in particular make writing electric: Morse, Baudot and Bemer. Morse represents a character with dots and dashes, Baudot with bits; and Bemer sets the number of bits in a character to eight (obsoleting many computers) and creates the ASCII alphabet (1960).

ASCII becomes the bloodstream of UNIX, which is built on textfiles, ASCII file paths and ASCII process intercommunication.

ASCII is now being replaced by Unicode, able to handle thousands of characters-- but which to choose? Language issues worldwide are now being decided by tekkie committees-- with a harsh impact on the traditions of many cultures.

The alphabet, upper and lower case came about by various accidents, as did their transmogrification into electronic form.

Human languages are of many kinds, and so are the writing systems we have devised— hieroglyphics, syllabaries, ideograms, phonetic alphabets. But the western-style phonetic alphabet is the form that runs the computer world—specifically the Latin or Roman alphabet. (This is called "romanji" in Japanese; romanji is actually a part of Japanese writing.)

Our alphabet derived from the Phoenician, evolving into Greek and Latin; Latin in turn diverged into different styles—the old capital letters, and among others, a scrunched-down style called Uncial.

Lower case was introduced under Charlemagne in the 800s. This was part of a grand intellectual movement. In what is called the Carolingian Renaissance, Latin was re-standardized as a universal language of Europe-- now Medieval Latin. This unification and standardization may have been the work of the monk

Alcuin, Charlemagne's top staff intellectual. As part of this standardization, upper-case letters were combined with uncial, which became lower case; the result was called Carolingian miniscule, and it led today's upper and lower case in a number of languages.

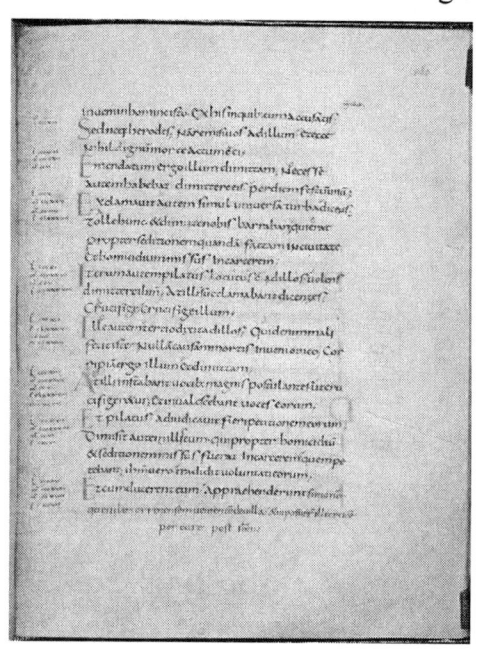

Carolingian upper and lower case.

WHAT WE WROTE ON. The first writing was on wax and stone, papyrus and parchment. Then, 2000 years ago, paper was introduced at the court of the Chinese emperor. It caught on only gradually. Brush and pen were the principal writing instruments until printing.
PRINT AND PRINTING PRESS. Wood-block printing was around for thousands of years (printing fabric in India, for instance), but movable type was invented in Korea before Gutenberg thought of it. Gutenberg created his own complete system, including means of casting metal type and ink that would adhere correctly to the type.

Gutenberg's Bible in 1439 revolutionized Europe. But Gutenberg went bankrupt, and scholars wonder what he was really aiming for.

Lehmann-Haupt, in *Gutenberg and the Master of the Playing Cards,* asserts that Gutenberg was going for high-quality illustrations, but his innovations were cut short.

It was Aldus Manutius who created the modern publishing industry and the personal book, printing hundreds of titles in Greek and introducing the font we now call *italic*. It can be argued that Manutius' personal book created the modern world.* The font called "Aldine" was supposedly created from the handwriting of the scholar Petrarch. Manutius is also said to have introduced the semicolon.

*Timothy Leary, personal communication.

THE TYPE FONT. A type font (fountain) was originally a box with many slots into which movable type was sorted. The term came to refer to whatever particular style and size was kept in one particular slotted box.

THE TYPEWRITER. There were basically two choices of writing until the late nineteenth century: handwriting, and the press. Then came the typewriter. Many competing typewriters were built in the 19th Century (Mark Twain was an early user.) The QWERTY keyboard, which everybody complains about, was designed to keep mechanical typewriters from jamming. If you want the supposedly-better Dvorak keyboard, you can remap it in software, but almost nobody does. (Witness the power of standardization.)

That QWERTY keyboard casts a long shadow. When ASCII (below) was defined, it became part of the computer universe. **QWERTY + ASCII** defined interaction for UNIX, and much that has followed in the world of personal software. QWERTY commands, made into sets of semi-symmetrical operations, exist for almost all programs, mouse-oriented or not.

COMPUTER KEYBOARDS. The IBM PC keyboard, originally 84 keys, was from the IBM System/23 Datamaster. It was later expanded to the present 104 keys. It is with us today in different variations. To ASCII it adds arrow keys, PgUp, PgDn, Enter and others. **RESULTS OF THE CONSTRUCT**: Most interaction on computers, even if there is a mouse, has character-control options, and they have been assigned to these keys in very particular ways—especially for selection and marking.

ELECTRICAL ALPHABETS. Then text was represented electrically. Three men in particular made writing electric: **Morse** represented a character with dots and dashes. **Baudot** put the character on parallel wires as a set of bits. **Bemer's fight.** There were dozens of competing computer alphabets,

¿**MYTH?** Baudot code was upper case because Baudot thought God required it.* Supposedly Baudot code was going to be all lower-case because it was more readable, till someone realized that would mean "god" (dieu) would be all lower case, and this would be sacriligeous; thus Baudot code was projected to an all-caps printer.

*We are still trying to track down the origin of this story.

but after huge political fights in the 1960s (especially with and amongst IBM), genial programmer-politician Bob Bemer managed to persuade part of the computer world to make the 8-bit byte the fundamental unit of information. Along with that he led the politics that created the ASCII alphabet code in 1963. ASCII was not generally adopted for years, but it became a fundamental part of Unix and gradually the center of computer communication. It also led to the redesign of much computer hardware (the System 360, the PDP-11, the 8008) and to Unix (below).

ASCII code set the number of bits in a character to eight, though only seven were used—they wanted a parity bit at that time. ("Bytes" had come in different lengths, usually six but sometimes settable, before that.) Making an eight-bit byte the standard character indirectly also made eight bits the standard unit of information storage and transmission, obsoleting many computers. It led to machines designed around 8 bits for everything: the IBM 360, PDP-11 and VAX. (Many important machines had a 36-bit structure, including the IBM 704-7090 series and DEC's PDP-6-10-20 series. These machines died.)

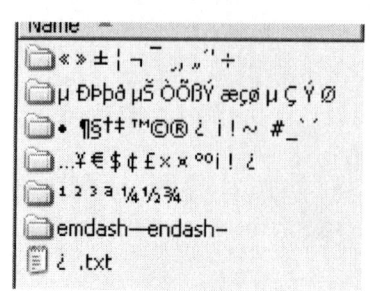

How certain fumy characters line up in Windows.

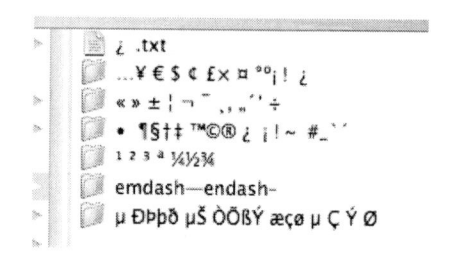

How the same characters line up on the Macintosh.

ASCII became a key aspect of Unix and thus of the whole computer world. Indeed ASCII is the bloodstream of UNIX, which is built on textfiles, communication between processes by ASCII text, and a central directory with files listed in ASCII.

THE UNICODE FIGHT, ACROSS THE WORLD

Other character sets, competing with ASCII, were adopted by Apple, by Microsoft and by various standards bodies; but finally now everybody is settling on Unicode.

ASCII is now being replaced by Unicode, able to handle thousands of characters-- but which? Unicode comes in several varieties, with up to 32 bits per character, which you would think would be enough—but God is in the details, as the Shakers originally said.

In every culture there are fights about language: tradition versus innovation, variant traditions, high culture versus slang and dialect. Usually these are settled by cultural mechanisms (growing and waning popularity), demographic mechanisms (growing and waning minorities) and sometimes legislation (e.g. the creation of "new Norwegian" in the 1940s).

Unfortunately, social and language issues are tied up with writing, and this means that key issues of cultures worldwide are being thrown to Unicode committees. Language issues worldwide are now being decided by tekkie committees-- with a harsh impact on the traditions of many cultures.

Normally these play out in literature and demography and local politics. (See proposed spelling reformations by George Bernard Shaw§ and Dolton Edwards.§) But having them controlled by the technical community puts things in a new and harsh footing.

This may be seen as the political simplification and deciding of all language issues worldwide by Geek Central— which is having harsh impact on the traditions of many cultures. The propaganda says how great it is, a glorious opening-up (since these languages can now have websites of their own that nobody can find with ASCII), and the damage is not mentioned, as it wipes out pockets of cultural memory everywhere.

Unicode violence to names in China. This example is from Reuters: "Sixty million Chinese [have] the problem that their names use ancient characters so obscure that computers cannot recognize them".

What does this actually mean? The phrasing is an outrageous propagandistic turn on the situation. The fact that the "ancient" characters aren't in Unicode means that those in charge of Unicode assignment have declined to include these characters in the new world, declaring them to be obscure, or whatever. A door has been closed on these people, their names and their lives. This may relate to Chinese politics or it may be guys in the back room; the important thing to realize is the cunning twist of meaning in the phrase "ancient characters so obscure that computers cannot recognize them".

HANDWRITING RECOGNITION. Handwriting recognition has been more difficult than many supposed. Of special interest is the system adopted by Palm, which did not recognize your handwriting but recognized your use of their cleverly-simplified system. The Palm Pilot originally had a writing system called Graffiti, beautifully designed by Jeff Hawkins, that allowed you to write with a stylus on the little screen. It was very elegant. Unfortunately a patent lawsuit from Xerox PARC required them to change it, so Graffiti 2, now supplied by Palm, is inferior. (Supposedly there are hacks that allow devotees to use the original.)

Chapter -25 Punctuation (ancient beginnings)

Summary. MEANWHILE, punctuation begins as a way of separating and clarifying. The innovations of space and period are followed by such helpers and conceits as comma, question mark, colon.

But what matters today are the accidental and committee decisions that select punctuation for the ASCII alphabet: the slash, the backslash, the @-sign, all of which take on special meaning. And through the structure of UNIX file search commands, some of the characters come to be unusable in filenames.

(But Unicode now allows lots of strange punctuation.)

Punctuation began as a way of separating, clarifying, later emphasizing. Early alphabetical writing was back-and-forth (boustrophodon) with no spaces or periods, which was disorienting and inconvenient. The innovations of space and period (and starting at one side only) were followed by such helpers as comma, question mark, colon, semicolon, ampersand (a visual contraction of the Latin word "et", meaning "and"), exclamation point, pilcrow, interrobang, irony point.

ASCII PUNCTUATION. What matters today are the committee decisions and accidents that got some punctuation into ASCII, which casts a long shadow over us today. Which punctuation made it into the ASCII computer alphabet?

space ! " # $ % & ' ( ) * + , - . / : ; < = > ? @ [\ ] ^ _ ` { | } ~

Well, most of these were on the standard American typewriter keyboard, except for

\ ~ < = > ^ | [ ] {}

All of these have been given very particular meanings, especially in file maintenance and programming languages.

@. The @-sign, which the French used centuries ago for prices and which was called "at" in English, made it into ASCII with the same price interpretation. But how'd it get into email addresses? It just happened to be there, and Ray Tomlinson saw in 1971 that it made a nice pun-- the person was "@" the specific address.

Backslash. Well, Bob Bemer took credit for putting the backslash in ASCII. Backslash as an override character became a part of the Unix input and text idiom. Paul Allen takes credit for changing the slash to backslash for the Microsoft path separator (thanks a lot!-- although it's not well known that you can use the forward slash as well).

Why all those parens? They sure liked parentheses.

()[]{}<>

No multiply. That there was no multiplication symbol added was interesting, since the other characters of standard arithmetic and algebra were present—

+ - / = ( )

Presumably the committee intended the asterisk to stand in for multiplication in order to make room for one of the other characters, but who knows now.

Forbidden characters in filenames. Why can't you use some characters in filenames? Specifically, in Windows you can't use

/ \ : * ? " < >

Why? Because they're query symbols, inherited from used in Unix for requesting and selecting files. Note that the Macintosh OS X gets

GEMS BEARING GIFTS 19

around this and allows all of these except the colon— but beware of moving the files to other systems.

QUESTIONABLE CONTENT. So how can you mark a file as questionable? Well, you can use the Spanish pre-question mark ¿.)

Those left behind. The punctuation marks that didn't make it into ASCII are amusing: for example, pilcrow (paramark), pointing finger, "therefore" symbol, "because" symbol. They didn't make it into ASCII-- but they later make it into Unicode! But not, alas, the Interrobang, the Irony Point, and other more charming/effete) punctuation proposals.

Irony point
(also called point d'ironie, snark or zing),
proposed by French poet
Alcanter de Brahm.

Chapter -24 Encryption (ancient beginnings)

Summary. Once there are alphabets you have more to hide. Julius Caesar does it. Edgar Allan Poe popularizes it. Kings, commoners, governments, armies encrypt their writings for thousands of years, but the early methods are pretty simple. The big breakthrough comes in the 1970s with trapdoor codes, which the U.S. government tries to suppress. The government gives up and now much private communication is based on trapdoor code-- secure socket transmission, digital signatures, intranets, firewalls and more.

But everyone's sure the NSA is ahead of us all.

The history of encryption has had a number of fascinating public events, while its greater successes probably remain secret.

The Zimmermann Telegram. In 1917, the U.S. was still outside World War I, but a key intercept may have tipped the balance and brought the U.S. into the war. This was the so-called Zimmermann telegram, decrypted by British code-breakers in their "Room 40". In the encoded telegram, Germany offered military aid to Mexico if they would only attack the U.S. to regain the states of Texas, New Mexico, and Arizona (lost a century before). Despite the inanity of this offer, the Zimmermann telegram created a spectacular uproar in the USA, which joined the war a month later.

The Stimson dictum. In 1929, Secretary of State Henry Stimson disbanded U.S. decryption facilities (the State Department's "Black Chamber") with his famous dictum that "gentlemen do not read other people's mail." But when Stimson took over as Secretary of War in 1940, his qualms on the matter were gone, and the U.S. was back in the decoding business.

CRYPTO IN WWII. In World War II, the U.S. broke the Japanese code (Purple) while our British Allies broke the German codes (Enigma, attacked by Turing's Bombe, and another rotary encryption machine with the less perky name of Lorenz SZ40/42, attacked by Flowers' Colossi). On the ground, U.S. forces in the South Pacific recruited Navaho speakers for reconnaissance (as celebrated in the film "Code Talkers").

VENONA. The Cold War quickly supplanted World War II, with new cryptographic challenges. The "Venona intercepts" in the 1940s and later indicated that there might be indeed some 350 Russian-controlled persons in the U.S. government, a figure which may have been leaked to Senator McCarthy as '400 Communists in the State Department', a number widely ridiculed at the time.

THE NSA, OUR EYES AND EARS ON THE WORLD. The National Security Agency, created in 1952, is a (seemingly) centralized facility for decrypting and analyzing foreign communications as they affect U.S. security. The size of the organization is not known, though observers have counted some 18,000 parking spaces on their main lot.

The NSA holds various secret, non-expiring patents, which can only be accidentally discovered when civilians apply to patent the same techniques.

THE TRAPDOOR BREAKTHROUGH OF THE 1970s. The big breakthrough came in the 1970s. In the old days, it was assumed that a code (or cipher) had to have one key, possessed by parties at both ends. But Rivest, Shamir and Adelman (RSA) proposed a public-key system. The idea was this: you could have two keys and only give one away, the public key; the other key you hold onto as a secret key. The two keys are symmetrical. Anyone can write to you using the public key, but only you can read the message, with the secret key. Conversely, you can write a public message, guaranteed to be from you, with the secret key-- Anyone can read it using the public key, but no one can fake such a message without the secret key. Not only did R, S and A come up with this idea, but they came up with the mathematics to support it, out of prime number theory.

RSA public-key code became a libertarian issue, because many people not only wanted privacy, but also the guaranteed digital signatures that that RSA promised. By government order declared secret, copies of the RSA papers circulated in samizdat, reaching everyone who cared in plain brown envelopes. The government backed off, and now look-- much private communication is based on trapdoor code. This includes secure socket transmission, digital signatures, intranets, firewalls and more.

Then an idealistic young guy named Phil Zimmermann built a trapdoor system for the public (Pretty Good Privacy, or PGP) and the official company tried to put him in jail; he used the press brilliantly, got media sympathy and won his case.

But of course everyone is sure the NSA is ahead of us all. The U.S. National Security Agency, charged with knowing about dangers and enemies, has since the 1950s had some of the hottest computers, notably IBM's HARVEST and who knows what today.

PORT KNOCKING,
A FORM OF SPREAD-SPECTRUM ENCRYPTION

Split-spectrum cryptography, as everyone knows, was co-invented by German expatriate movie star Hedy Lamarr (who hated Hitler and wanted to do her part) and her friend composer George Antheil. (Antheil was a veteran of the Paris avant-garde, a friend of Stravinsky and Joyce; his musical piece *Ballet Mécanique* (1924) had made him "the bad boy of music", a tough distinction to hold onto.)

Hedy: What's that knocking?

Their idea was simple: you send your broken parts of your message on several different channels, and the adversary doesn't know when or where to look. The Lamarr-Antheil patent showed a little music-box inside a torpedo; this was much derided by the military, but their method is now used extensively. (They weren't the only ones to invent this-- earlier patents had been granted to Telefunken engineers—but we honor their grit and determination.)

The latest variation on this is called Port Knocking. When there is heavy traffic or demand on a software port, a signal can be sent to *another* port to say something is coming in that should be answered. The principle of mixing your message among different channels is the same that Hedy advocated much earlier.

-23 Making Documents Hierarchical (18th Century)

Summary. The French *philosophes* and Encyclopedists sought to put all knowledge into sequence and hierarchy, as did Dewey's with his decimal system.

Since the World Wide Web, hierarchy has been imposed on documents several different ways: the exposed hierarchies of the directories and pages; internal hierarchical markup (HTML, XML); and Cascading Style Sheets. There will undoubtedly be more. But how much violence does this do to the content?

Before the French revolution there was a great flowering of intellect, carefully supervised by the King's secret police, that greatly moved modern science along—creating the metric system in a land that still had kings and nobles. These French *philosophes* and Encyclopedists sought to put all knowledge into sequence and hierarchy. This seemed especially appropriate in the eighteenth century, when Linnaeus created the great taxonomic system for plants and animals; he thought everything was hierarchical, including fire and rocks. However, it worked for plants and animals because hierarchy was imposed, but because it was the actual structure of the domain.

Hierarchy was a useful way to organize a big book; it was also helpful for organizing libraries, as did Melvil Dewey with his library decimal system. But it was only very approximate. You can make a hierarchy of topics, like the Dewey Decimal System, but you can't make a document be about just one topic, and the more general the document the less sense such assignment makes— especially since categories keep changing, splitting, and appearing out of nowhere.

ARE DOCUMENTS INTRINSICALLY HIERARCHICAL? That is up to each author. The Harvard outline, in the 20th Century, has had a powerful influence; people are told that organizing hierarchically is "thinking logically", though it means cutting many connections and associations to select a few. Many technical people believe this is correct and necessary. However, essayists work differently. Technical documents may be traditionally hierarchical, but novels and filmscripts and poems are not. History and essays are somewhere between, with expository arcs, punch points and harmonics of exposition. Free-form prose writing (such as the superb writing in the *New Yorker*) follow rambling sequences, chosen by the author, with novel-like arcs, punches and stings.

"MARKUP". Originally markup meant physical markings, often in red or blue pencil, on a manuscript— to indicate changes, or give instructions to a typesetter. But this shifted to markup meaning "data structure for applying fonts to characters", and got tangled with the text content itself. Text attributes were represented inside a file— in data structures that wrapped around words and phrases. This ugly mechanism, rendering the content unreadable and unfit for other uses, has been glorified and extended in a chain—GML (IBM's General Markup Language), SGML (STANDARDIZED General Markup Language), HTML (HyperText Markup Language), and now XML (Tim Bray) for the cosmic hierarchical representation of everything. All of these use markup codes scrambled inside the contents of the documents, rather than cleanly on the side, which is directly equivalent but much cleaner.

Additional "MARKUP LANGUAGES". This mechanism of wrapping content with parenthetical markers is a great favorite in the technical community; literally hundreds of markup languages have been built, with the intention of representing every subdomain by commangling its data with identifiers.

THE WEB'S HIERARCHIES. The World Wide Web imposes hierarchy on documents in at least three different ways. The directories of the Internet; the HTML encoding of the Web file; Cascading Style Sheets (Håkon Lie). There are undoubtedly more.

THE PROBLEM. Any imposed template is oppressive. Hierarchy should be an option, not an imposition.

Chapter -22 They All Invented Computers   (hardware) (1822)

Summary.   A crabby London generalist, a genial physicist with a squad of brilliant youngsters, the Bletchley Park crypto team, a high-school kid collaborating with an engineer he met on CB radio-- all come separately to the concept of a machine that follows a plan, misnamed "computer".

But who should get the prize? Perhaps the little-known businessman-scientist who is first to create a working programmable digital computer, and first to use binary numbers on a computer-- all under the nose of the Nazis. (Plus the first to design a computer language.)

CHARLES BABBAGE, a mathematician, generalist and Fellow of the Royal Society, came upon the idea of a machine to do repetitive calculations, probably in 1822. After working on this Difference Engine for years, he realized there could be a far *better* machine which would be run by a changeable stored program (the Analytical Engine). He told the government funders that he should stop and build that machine instead. This was a mistake. (His first machine was completed only recently, and guess what? It works just fine.) Babbage would yell at traveling musicians under his window, making his window a popular location for the British busker to visit.

> John Walker has not only written wonderful stuff about the Analytical Engine, he has created an analytical engine **EMULATOR**!
> See fourmilab.ch/babbage §

KONRAD ZUSE was a German engineer-businessman whose work is too little appreciated. His first computer, the Z1 (built in his parents' apartment), did not work correctly, but it was programmable and was the first binary computer. He built the world's first working programmable computer, the Z3, in 1941, with a program read from punch tape. He created one of the first computer startup companies (1948) and published the first design for a computer language, Plankalkül, in the same year. (In 1969 he wrote a book proposing that the universe is digital, an idea later expanded by Fredkin and Wolfram.)

(**VANNEVAR BUSH** built an analog computer at MIT in the 1930s, but we're not counting analog here.)

HOWARD AIKEN. Aiken got the idea of an automatic calculator as an engineering student, probably in the late 1930s. Fortunate enough to have a long-term career at Harvard and funding from IBM, he built the electro-mechanical Mark I (1944), the Mark II, III and IV-- the last being fully electronic, with drum and core memories. His work gets far less attention that that of Mauchly and Eckert.

JOHN MAUCHLY AND J. PRESPER ECKERT, a genial physicist and hotshot kid, along with a string of *more* hotshot kids, built the Eniac computer in secret during World War II at the University of Pennsylvania. It was intended to calculate ballistic trajectories and finally did, but had no effect on the war. (Why was it so secret when Aiken's very similar work was right out in public? These things are mysteries.) Mauchly originally hoped to use the computer for his intended physics research, but never did.

> FEUD: Mauchly raged at von Neumann for having published their idea without attribution-- 'We were under military security, he wasn't, and they told us to tell him everything!' But his anger was greater at the historian who promoted von Neumann as the originator of the idea.*
>
> *John Mauchly, personal communication.

Note that the ENIAC was 30 by 60 feet, had 18,000 vacuum tubes, could store only 20 numbers, and took 200,000 man-hours to build. (Today's wristwatch has more circuitry.)

After the war they started their own computer company, which became Univac.

TOMMY FLOWERS and his code-breaking team at Bletchley Park built a secret fleet of general-purpose computers. (For some reason Flowers worked for the Post Office.) Whereas Turing and his group (in another department at Bletchley Park) had created a special-purpose machine called The Bombe to crack the Enigma codes of the U-boats, the Colossus machines were much more general and used to crack codes from the Lorenz Machine, a tougher German code machine to break than Enigma but based on the same principle (stepping wheels).

The first Colossus worked in December 1943, so some argue that it may have been the first operational general-purpose computer (the competitor being Zuse).

The Colossus machine (a picture that somehow survived).

Colossi were run in parallel on different parts of a problem. After the war the Colossus machines were smashed on Churchill's instructions. The very existence of the Colossus computers remained a secret until the 1970s, by which time you could buy the equivalent of a Colossus as a personal computer.

(**GEORGE STIBITZ**, often in such computer-inventor lists, did not build a general-purpose programmable computer, nor did **JOHN VINCENT ATANASOFF**, declared in court to be the official inventor of computers.)

¿**HOW COME?** Why is it that the wartime work of Eckert & Mauchly and the Colossus group were top secret, even though Howard Aiken was doing essentially the same stuff in the open? We may never know.

Chapter -21 They All Idealized Computers (1843)

Summary. There is another way to invent computers: to envision a magical unified ideal. There are many ways you can think about the computer— any of which can be enacted in software. Each offers a different style of use and a different kind of computer life.

Different people see computers differently from the beginning, and describe their idealized sytems. Abstract visions of the computer are advanced by Lord Byron's daughter, a sexually indiscreet U-boat hunter, a Hungarian from the Manhattan Project, a lady admiral, a Norwegian politician-puppeteer, not to mention various mathematicians and engineers. All these ideas are correct, but each determines what you do with the computer.

Like the blind men and the elephant, none of them is wrong, but unlike the blind men, some of them get to build the elephant to their own specifications.

The All-Purpose Machine. (Augusta Ada King, Countess of Lovelace; John von Neumann.) We know that Von Neumann, in the 1940s, was the first to call the computer an all-purpose machine, but the person who knew it first was Ada Lovelace. She was Lord Byron's daughter, and perhaps brought a touch of his poetry to her acute scientific work. Ada Lovelace was the first to see and elucidate the vast possibilities of Babbage's Analytical Engine-- predicting practical uses as well as scientific-- including computer graphics and automatic musical composition.

But she went further. Even though the Analytical Engine never worked, she wrote the first program for it-- and in the process discovered the subroutine.

An abstract repetitive machine. (Alan Turing.) The story in brief: An unusual young mathematician considered which problems could actually be solved by a long series of operations, and which ones could never be figured out.

This abstract machine—declared to have a recording tape, something that would appear much later, except Turing's was infinite-- became considered a fundamental mathematical entity. The Turing-machine is a mathematical abstraction that defines what can be done. This abstract machine has some properties of real computers, but no practical applications (given that we pretty much know now what's doable). Turing went on to make crucial discoveries in cracking "Enigma", the Nazi codebox that controlled the subs in the Atlantic, possibly winning WW II.

¿WHATIF? Without Turing, would the allies have broken the U-boat blockade? It is fortunate that Turing was not blocked by his homosexuality from secret government work, as many were later; we might have lost the war. It is less fortunate that he was arrested for loitering in a Manchester men's room, which led to his suicide.

¿HOW COME? LITTLE-KNOWN FACT: How did Turing get his own name on "The Turing Machine," when academics can't name things after themselves? **Answer**: he sent his paper to his good friend Alonzo Church, who published it and coined the term "Turing machine" for his benefit.*

*Andrew Hodges, personal communication.

DISCOVERY OF THE ALGORITHM. The algorithm, or transposable symbolic method*, is attributed jointly to Alan Turing and Emil Post in 1936.

*My definition, which I hope you appreciate.

Note that "algorithm" is actually someone's *name*. It is named after a Persian mathematician, Al-Khwārizmī who wrote a book on calculating with Hindu numerals in 825. His name became "algorithm".

The "von Neumann Machine". JOHN von NEUMANN, a mathematician and generalist who worked on the first atomic bomb, is credited with a principal abstraction of the computer-- the idea of storing both data and programs in the same memory. This is because of a widely-circulated memorandum he wrote in 1946. However, the idea had been thought of by Eckert and Mauchly before him, as well as by Konrad Zuse and (in more abstract form) by Turing.

Monopoly by sales and technical teams and captive computer centers. (Thomas J. Watson.) Watson defined IBM; the IBM spirit and organization were his, and this strange form of monopoly just followed from the way the company was run—an astonishing system that was probably not thought out explicitly.

Computer for higher mathematics, and oh yeah, fooling around. (John McCarthy, Gerald Sussman.) Based on Alonzo Church's lambda-calculus, McCarthy's Lisp language was intended for mathematics and general use; it became the basic language for hacking in the original sense (experimenting and fooling around). It has fewer restrictions than any other language, and is built into Emacs. Sussman's Scheme language corrects a fundamental defect in Lisp that almost no one is aware of, and few are capable of understanding.

Engineering machine. (John Backus.) John Backus's idea: the computer does lots of engineering calculations with a lot of numbers ("number crunching"). Backus created Fortran, a language to optimize fast floating-point array calculations. Like all successful languages, it became general-purpose; now in general disuse, Fortran lives on as the standard supercomputer language.

Algorithmic machine. (Turing, Wirth, Knuth.) Emphasizing the notion of mathematical algorithms, founded by Turing, Niklaus Wirth creates a series of languages (especially ALGOL) to facilitate transposition and generalization of mathematical methods. This work was continued by Donald Knuth, whose style of systematization was revealed when he published, "The Potrzebie System of Weights and Measures" in *Mad* magazine, while he was in college. His sequel, *Fundamental Algorithms*, runs to several volumes, and in the course of creating it he had to build his own typesetting software, TeX, which has a great following.

One-Person Computer: (Wes Clark, Ken Olsen.) Wes Clark built the one-person computer, the LINC, at MIT, and seeded them to labs around the country in the early sixties. Meanwhile, based on Clark's digital modules, a company called Digital Equipment Corporation, run by Ken Olsen from beginning to end, introduced the one-person commercial computer. DEC was a wonderful little company that specialized in easy-to-use machines, starting in 1960. Unfortunately Olsen later could not imagine or move toward the huge personal market, and indignantly said DEC computers would never be used for games— little knowing, or perhaps not admitting, that the very first computer games had been developed on DEC machines.

Elegant notational machine. Ken Iverson's APL language, built around an extraordinary (and fundamentally simple) notation of his own devising, created great loyalty among those who learned programming from it, or physics (from John Boccio's pioneering APL-based physics course at Swarthmore). Alas, this elegant system could not hold its niche; it was seen as a cliquish and obscure system, whereas it was incredibly general.

Time-Sharing Machine: (Corbato, Kemeny). Fernando Corbató at MIT pioneered the Compatible Time-Sharing System (CTSS) at MIT, 1961. John Kemeny at Dartmouth made the time-sharing computer the backbone of the university, and was elevated from professor to president. It would be decades before most of the world would catch up with Dartmouth's level of access.

Secure computing: (Tony Hoare, Norm Hardy, Mark Miller, Jonathan Shapiro.) C.A.R. "Tony" Hoare, in England, designed the computer language OCCAM and the Transputer computer chip for secure computing. Unfortunately this superbly-thought-out work did not catch on. Norm Hardy originally patented what some say is the most secure method for computing: the capability-based system. Carnegie-Mellon did hardware experiments on capability systems in the 1970s. Now an experimental language (E, created by Mark Miller) and an experimental operating system (EROS, created by Jonathan Shapiro) are building capability into software. This may be the only way out of our extremely vulnerable network world. (See Malware.) Miller hopes E will get us out of the "Turing tarpit" of essentially equivalent languages with a fundamentally different model.

Computer as Intercommunications Network, Especially for Communicating Among People. (J.C.R. "Lick" Licklider, Bob Taylor, Larry Roberts, Paul Baran...) See ARPANET.

Simulation machine for armies of imaginary robots. (Kristen Nygaard, pron. "nugard".) Nygaard was a politician and a computer scientist, as well as having taken Agnar Mykle's puppeteering course.* "I kept Norway out of the E.U.", he would say proudly.* In order to handle rich simulations of multiple thingies, Nygaard and Dahl invented object-oriented programming with the Simula language (see Object-Oriented Programming).

*Kristen Nygaard, personal communication.

Computer for kids. (Alan Kay.) In the seventies and eighties, Alan Kay tireless campaigned for children's having computers to program.

Computer as fashion accessory. (Steve Jobs.) Under Jobs' cunning vision, the Macintosh became not just a fashion accessory, but an identity statement-- "I'm creative!" This was brilliant marketing.

Computer as casual programming system. (Larry Wall.) Wall's Perl language, called "the duct tape of the Internet", is based on his slogan, "There's more than one way to do it". Fans of elegant programming languages hate it, but it gets the job done.

Chapter -20 Database (1884)
(1884 was the date of Hollerith's patent application.)

Summary. Keep track of everything by computer!-- always the dream of both management and hobbyists. Just a small problem of specifics.

Automatic databasing starts with a doctor and a mining engineer, leading to punch cards, in the 1890 census, leading to IBM and its 80-column mentality. Relational Database (now standard) is designed by a feisty Oxford mathematician-RAF pilot who insists on thirteen axioms (called his "12 rules"), which are now universally ignored. He is appalled by the SQL language which IBM later develops (now standard). Meanwhile, Object-Oriented databases fit better with today's computer languages-- but nobody can agree on their structure.

The real problem is: for databases to be universal and shared, everyone has to agree not just on the structure, but on the categories and terminology (now called Ontologies), for all time. Uh-huh. Or trust committees for that. Uh-huh. But there's a big German company that will take care of you, promising that all databases in your company VILL work together.

A database is any principled arrangement of information that you can look things up in.* Naturally it was always everybody's dream: one place to put information, accessible from all over! We'd use computers to keep track of *everything*! And send lists to each other! Just a small problem of specifics. And standardization.

*My definition, which I hope you appreciate.

The doctor, the mining engineer, and tab cards. Herman Hollerith was a mining engineer living in Manhattan (where there are not many mines). The idea of counting holes electrically was suggested to Hollerith by John Shaw Billings, creator of the New York Public Library and the National Library of Medicine, who had been a surgeon in the Civil War. Hollerith turned his attention from holes in the ground to holes in cards.   Hollerith's patented punch cards counted and tabulated the 1890 census. IBM was founded on that invention, and only slowly moved from a punch-card view of data and its maintenance.

The mainframe era: What wasn't a database? In the mainframe era, 1947-87, everything was implicitly a database; only gradually did the database become a separate concept. Data had "indexes", points of entry which led to individual records, as in ISAM (Indexed Sequential Access Method) and related concepts.

Relational Database, (which now runs the commercial world) was designed by Edgar Codd, a feisty Oxford mathematician and RAF pilot who insisted on thirteen axioms (called his "12 rules"), which are now universally ignored. At one time he had 500 IBMers working under him; but he was then told he had to deliver product in two years.* He left IBM in a huff, and was appalled by the SQL language which IBM then developed (now standard-- possibly because it provides a first line of defense against programmer embezzlement, which had already begun in the '60s).   Oracle, through fierce salesmanship, is the leader of relational database now.

```
                *Anonymous IBMer, personal communication.
```

Object-Oriented Databases. Meanwhile, object-oriented databases fit better with today's computer languages. But nobody can agree on their structure. Furthermore, OO imposes hierarchy and hierarchical access, which Relational Database does not.

THE LURKING PROBLEM: For databases to be universal and shared, everyone has to agree not just on the structure, but on the categories and terminology (now called Ontologies—a term from philosophy meaning "the study of existence"). But the problem is that we have to agree on the categories and terminology for all time. (Are you laughing yet? This concept is called, among other things, the Semantic Web.) Of course, instead of agreeing for all time, delegating our language to hundreds of committees will do nicely, or so the tekkies think.

If all this is too daunting, a big German company called SAP will take care of all databasing for a corporation. However, this requires that all accounting (and essentially all methods within the organization) follow the SAP blueprint. You just have to do everything their way, in every detail. Enjoy.

MIS. Management Information Systems, or MIS, was a hope (or slogan) starting in the nineteen-sixties. The idea is that all up-to-the-minute corporate information will be directly available to management, on screen, any time. This is not what has happened so far. A new term, or perhaps similar movement, is **data warehousing**, yet another methodology for keeping track of stuff that has not fully caught on.

COMBINING DATABASES. Perhaps the dirtiest secret in the business information world is how hard it is to combine databases, especially when two companies merge. The slightest differences have enormous consequences. The easiest way is to start over, which is impossible.

The most extraordinary achievement in this area is by Bob Carlson (see Ch. 20).

Chapter -19   Voting Machines (1892)

Summary.   The original voting machine of 1892 could be examined by anybody to verify its fair operation. No more. Several brands of electronic voting machine have now been widely deployed in the USA, all questionable.

It's best to think of an electronic voting machine as a video game—it's impossible to know the real rules, you can just hope.

Mechanical voting machines, starting in 1892, were designed to be easily understood and guaranteed fair because anyone could see they were fair.

No longer.   Today's friendly-looking voting machine could be a total fraud, and there is no way that certification methods by mere testing can find out.

Knowledgeable people* keep trying to fight these machines, trying to tell Americans that today's "electronic voting machines" are *intrinsically* dishonest, in that no technical verification exists, or possibly can. To verify the software would take a deep clean-room, white/black-hat operation; to actually verify each unit in the field would take a big team with metal detectors and heavy gear.

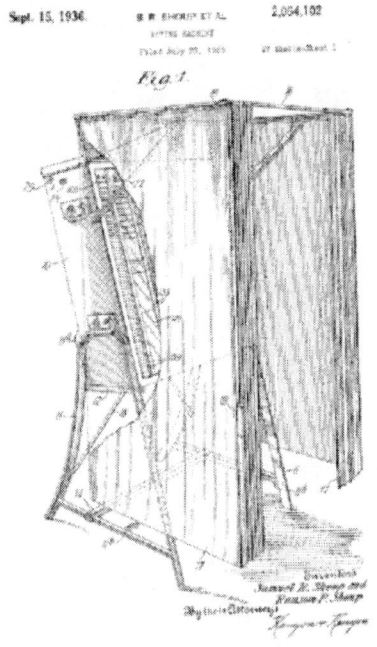

```
         * Notably Barbara Simons (past president of the ACM,
         the world society of computer scientists), and The
         Electronic Frontier Foundation (the premier civil
         liberties organization in the computer field).
```

Yet these machines are "verified" by apparently-clueless certification committees who study how they respond. But any computer scientist, hacker or teenage programmer can tell you that no amount of studying its external behavior will tell you what it's going to do on election day.

The electronic voting machine is best understood as a video game programmed to look like a democratic input device. (In video games, someone else has created a world you can only guess at.) In the future we may never know the true vote count, just what some hidden technician tells these machines to report.

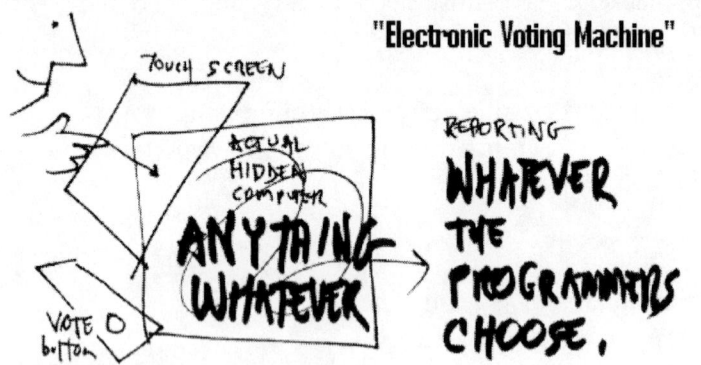

"Electronic Voting Machine"
TOUCH SCREEN
ACTUAL HIDDEN COMPUTER
REPORTING WHATEVER THE PROGRAMMERS CHOOSE.
ANYTHING WHATEVER
VOTE O button

There is no reason that anyone in the chain—from the head of the voting machine company down to a sneaky technician— cannot set the results.

The manufacturers won't show EFF the internal code-- though Security guys today believe that any security relying on secret programs isn't secure at all.

> No one ever went broke underestimating the intelligence of the American public.
> H.L. Mencken

People are treating this as a mere technical issue. It's not. It's an issue that strikes at the heart of democracy. The potentially dishonest use of these machines expands the range of options and considerations vastly— on both sides. It's both technical and strategic: voting systems must be designed not just for friendly use but must be provably safe against adversarial attacks. It's the difference between hiring an engineer and a night watchman. You know someone may be out to break in and you must take many precautions, especially precautions the crooks won't know about. It's the same as the fight against Internet breakins (see Malware, Chapter 1.)

No one has gone so far as to say that Diebold or the others are deliberately fraudulent, in order to elect their own candidates, but it is certainly possible technically. This is the issue that confronts anyone trying to assure an honest voting system.

Chapter -18 Intellectual property (1923)

(Why the date, 1923? Recent "Sonny Bono" extensions to the copyright law seemingly lock everything since 1922 into copyright forever.)

Summary.   Intellectual property issues have been waiting for us all along, especially copyright and patent (among many branches of intellectual property law).

Copyright determines the legal right to copy. Anyone may hold a copyright, including artists, writers and big companies.

Today on the Internet, an us-versus-them attitude has developed, where ripping off copyrighted material from big companies has become a sport (first through Napster, now the ingenious BitTorrent, which is said to occupy a large part of world bandwidth). The big companies have responded with the Digital Millennium Copyright Act (whose safe-haven provisions make ISPs able to operate), Digital Rights Management (which is an unworkable mess) and lawsuits against people who least expect it.

Meanwhile, Apple's clever Ipod system has won big. The Ipod has to be downloaded through their Itunes program, which has provided a major sale gateway for content.

Intellectual property has always been a branch of law, and its issues have been waiting for the computer world all along.

> **THE COVER OF THIS BOOK:**
> **AN EXAMPLE OF MULTIPHASIC INTELLECTUAL PROPERTY.**
>
> Intellectual property is a many-sided problem. Just look at the front of this book. What rights issues are there? The cover of this book falls under at least four headings in intellectual property law.
>
> 1. **The copyright issue.** The Bill Gates mugshot everyone loves was taken by the Albuquerque police department and is thus adjudged to be in the public domain. See discussion at
> http://commons.wikimedia.org/wiki/Image:Bill_Gates_mugshot.png
>
> 2. **Personality rights.** You control the use of your picture for those purposes in which you might voluntarily offer it—appearing in a movie or endorsing a product. However, this is not such a situation.
>
> 3. **Privacy rights.** Most people have certain privacy rights, which extend into public places. This does not apply, however, to someone who has become a "public person", whether voluntarily or not. As a public person, Bill Gates cannot protest this.
>
> 4. **But will he sue? (Always the biggest issue in intellectual property cases.)** Niceties of the law aside, anyone can sue anyone for anything, however wrongfully, and those with money often win without grounds. Here's our judgment call: he probably won't, based on old friendship, the likelihood that he'll be amused, and the fact that this book tries to tell his story fairly.

Having to tell tekkies about intellectual property law is like having to tell small children about death: they put their hands over their ears and yell and jump up and down. They want to invent the way it should be in their minds (don't we all).

There are many forms of intellectual property-- copyright, patent, trade mark, service mark, trade secret, privacy, personality rights and lots more. All have particular rules and procedures. We'll only talk about copyright here except for one example, the cover (see box).

The laws of intellectual property have not simply been imposed from above; they clarify basic understandings shared everywhere. Intellectual property law, like other property law, provides guidelines to make traditions more precise. Rules that determine the ownership of a cow, boundaries of a field, etc. allow people to go about their lives knowing what to expect.

As with cows, so with trademarks and clown outfits. Before written law there were unwritten codes of intellectual property, which still exist in many areas. Clowns, for example, have even today an unwritten code about not stealing each others' makeup or gags; IP laws clarify such traditions.

COPYRIGHT

Copyright conveys the legal right to copy. Anyone may hold a copyright, including artists, writers and big companies. But the big companies have not really joined with the artists and writers, because the big companies are used to ripping the artists and writers off.

Another party in the equation is the public, who were quick to see that they could share music and videos on the net; the Internet is neutral and does not see what's happening in the packets.

Here are a few main copyright issues and events, briefly stated.

STEALING; or, ahem, Exchanging Files. Methods soon sprang up for exchanging files, often illegally, through peer-to-peer methods. 19-year-old "Napster" Fanning created a clever download system but he crossed the line legally, barely got out of the situation. Among other systems, the big winner was the politically and technically brilliant BitTorrent, created by Bram Cohen, who made sure it had thoroughly legitimate uses as well as being highly efficient for illegal file transfer. BitTorrent downloads are rumored to be a significant portion of Internet traffic.

ANGER ON BOTH SIDES. Response of publishers has been harsh, and so have reactions of Internet hotheads, saying they'll steal everything and bring down the copyright system.

UNILINEAR REACTION OF PUBLISHERS. Imagining no way to redefine the situation (such as microsale), publishers have responded with Draconian punishments and attempts at technical lockdown (Digital Rights Management, or DRM).

GEEKS BEARING GIFTS

DRM. DRM, or Digital Rights Management, is any attempt by technical means to restrict access to restricted content. Generally this is in the client, i.e. the user's machine. (Trying to prevent transmission of copyrighted materials on the Net is dubious at best).

In various forms, restriction of use by technical means (DRM) has been in the field since the beginning. Unix had Execute Permission separate from Read Permission, so you could run a program with no access to its content. In the dinky era, when programmers had greater control over disk drives, tricks were used to make files uncopiable-- placing the disk tracks in unconventional locations, for instance.

Today's DRM can only work certain ways, and many of them restrict normal functioning and slow the machine greatly. This is a principal reason for the terrible problems of Windows Vista. It was also a terrible gaffe by Sony, who created a piece of software referred to as the Sony Rootkit. It invaded your computer—a computer virus—when you played a Sony CD; and after that it interfered in various ways with proper functioning of the machine. In other words, it was a virus from a company. In the face of public horror, Sony stopped and supposedly recalled the CDs.

DRM ON DVDs. There was no DRM on CDs, but when the DVD was standardized, they made them uncopiable—supposedly. **LITTLE-KNOWN FACT:** Everyone knows that the DVD encryption was broken by Jon Lech Johansen, a 21-year-old Norwegian programmer. (Prosecuted in Norway, he got off on all charges.) It is not well known that the DVD encryption was intentionally made light by the DVD encryption committee, based arguments in a libertarian book, *Computer Lib*, published in 1974.* Johansen was very talented, but he went through a door that had been left ajar.

*Personal communication from member of committee who wishes to remain anonymous.

"Free Speech Flag," which has Secret DVD encryption key built into its colors.

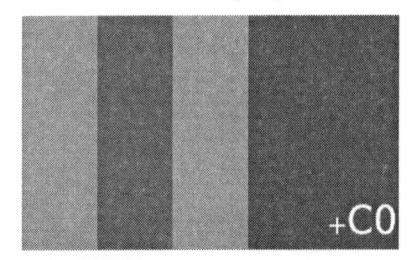

+C0

DRM THROUGH THE WEB BROWSER. As defined by Bina and Andreessen (see Ch. 14), the Web browser only provided content which could be downloaded—and if not explicitly kept by the user through a 'Save' command, could be pulled out of the browser cache (like various Flash objects).

No longer. Now it is possible to show things in the Web browser that the user can't keep, except through laborious screen shots. Partly through programming techniques called Ajax, the browser can window content that the user can't save. Not just YouTube, but Google Maps (try saving the data!), Amazon's peekaboo looks into available books, and various academic presses, and now the New Yorker.

> **END OF THE ERA OF MEDIA OWNERSHIP?**
>
> In a sense, this is the end of the era of Aldus Manutius (creator of the Personal Book) and Erasmus, symbol of the Renaissance, who said: "When I have money I buy books; if there is any left over I buy food and clothing."

THE DMCA. The Digital Millennium Copyright Act (1996) is a seemingly punitive piece of legislation, setting out explicit penalties for copyright violation. However, it has a vital "safe haven" provision holding ISPs harmless for content posted illegally, as long as they took it down on complaint, called a DMCA Takedown Notice. (Without such a proviso, the Internet would have come to an abrupt halt.) That provision is now being gamed with many frivolous takedown notices.

THE RIAA LAWSUITS. The RIAA (Recording Industry Association of America) has been suing individuals for downloading songs, demanding $750 per download. (Brad Templeton of the Electronic Frontier Foundation calls this "spamigation", or spam litigation.) The RIAA is doing immense harm to its own cause by suing various fragile individuals.

PUSHING THE BOUNDARIES OF FAIR USE. In another area, many parties are trying to erode copyright law by pushing the boundaries of fair use. (So much is posted that the publishers can't chase.)

SPECIAL LICENSES; CREATIVE COMMONS. Inspired by the effectiveness of the different open source licenses, a number of different copyright licenses are proposed for writings and other work. Most conspicuous among these is Larry Lessig's Creative Commons. Creative Commons is legally sound and excellently thought out, but doesn't necessarily do what people think. Best understood in the context of the open source community, Creative Commons is designed to sort out the options for small publishers. However, it doesn't help shake things loose from BIG publishers.

While it provides a number of different content licenses, they are likely to be used only by small publishers who wouldn't sue infringers anyway. The Creative Commons licenses will not be adopted by any of the big publishers, and it is loosening their content that is the real issue.

Other such content licenses include some that are pretty strange. For instance, the GNU Free Documentation License (often put on Wikipedia pictures), grants permission "to copy, distribute and/or modify this document under the terms ... with no Invariant Sections, no Front-Cover Texts, and no Back-Cover Texts." Whatever that is supposed to mean, it seems to forbids incorporating the pictures in anything else.

NON-CONFRONTATIVE SALE
Meanwhile, ignoring the controversies, some people have been creating sales methods that work. In particular—
    IPOD/ITUNES. The Apple approach has been less heavy-handed than the RIAA's, through the two-prong technique of Ipod and Itunes. The Ipod is set up so it will not play any content not downloaded from the Itunes program on your Macintosh (and more recently, PC). Itunes serves as a gateway to your Ipod.

MICROSALE AND MICROPURCHASE. But no one considers micropurchase of media by the selected portion-- which might be the general solution everyone's missed and no one recognizes.

While whole documents are sold on the Web, there is no system yet for the microsale of portions of content, and no clients or applications that can track, respect and work with it. This would be beneficial to small rightsholders and would motivate the big publishers to make their content more fluidly available, purchasable in small portions. It could make 'Mashup' would be legal. (This has always been the Xanadu proposal, see Chapter -11).

But the Web browser cannot assemble content pieces or cache owned portions. It may take Google's new deal with the publishing industry to make this method possible.

Chapter -17 The Mainframe Era

Summary. After developing the ENIAC during the war, Eckert and Mauchly get backing from Remington Rand (under the name Univac). Seeing this, IBM quickly takes over most of the computer business in the 1950s through its ferocious salesmanship. IBM arranges for computers to be run by vast teams in big bureaucracies, which they control. That system lasts some thirty years.

Also in the 1950s, real-time computers with graphics are built for air traffic control and running the nuclear war that doesn't happen. These developments seep through to the civilian sector, with minicomputers and graphic displays from DEC and others. But it's a small part of the market.

After the 8-bit byte is established by Bemer as the fundamental unit of information, IBM throws out its old 36-bit machines and brings out the 360 series, announced 1964. This hugely enlarges the market, but still dominated by computer centers brainwashed by IBM. Other manufacturers follow with 8-bit machines. But none of them imagines what's coming.

Computers were called "mainframes" from the late forties till the seventies, after which smaller ones began to sneak in, pretending to be non-threatening "microcomputers". (At first like little mammals eating dinosaur eggs, not disturbing the main food chain.)

IBM. Before computers there was a lot of other digital stuff, mainly controlled by IBM. Hollerith's punch cards (predecessor to IBM) organized the 1890 census. The equipment for punching and counting became the Computing Tabulating Recording Corporation company, then the International Business Machines Corporation. IBM was run with sanctimonious ferocity by Thomas J. Watson, an awesome personality who combined business toughness with a religious style of corporate organization.

Numbers and names on cards were being counted, sorted and tabulated by IBM equipment, especially in the 1930s-- for the administration of Roosevelt's New Deal, but even for the Nazis, a connection which IBM chooses to forget. (Watson sent back his Nazi medal, which was symbolically correct.)

THE STORY IN BRIEF: After the war, Eckert and Mauchly set up the Eckert and Mauchly Computer Company to commercialize their ENIAC computer.

So Eckert and Mauchly took their ENIAC computer—not the machine, of course, but the concept-- to IBM. Watson himself threw them out, according to legend, saying IBM already had computers (meaning tabulating machines, and their backing for Aiken at Harvard). The Eckert and Mauchly Computer Company was backed by Remington Rand under a new name, Univac. (Their punch cards were the same size as IBM's, but the holes were round.)

Watson responded quickly and created a computer division for IBM after all. Through its ferocious salesmanship, IBM quickly took over most of the business. They arranged for IBM computers to be run by vast teams in big bureaucracies, which they controlled.

(Computers for business, as then interpreted by IBM and Univac, often still keep track of information that was originally sliced to fit onto 80-column cards.)

The first commercial computers had less logic circuitry than today's digital wristwatch, far less than today's personal computers; and they used vacuum tubes, which were very unreliable.

It was now the early 1950s. (Note the Spencer Tracy film of those days, "The Desk Set", which tried to interpret all this.)

Systems also were built for air traffic control, with some of the first real-time displays. Other, scarier systems were built for Norad nuclear central in Cheyenne Mountain, both for warning and for the control of forces ("Command and Control"). Operation Chromedome (depicted in the film "Dr. Strangelove") kept a constant circulation of fully-thermonuclear B-52s constantly circulating the periphery of the Soviet Union. These vast forces had to be set up, maintained and tracked. This meant computers, and thank god, they worked.

THE 8-BIT CHANGE. After the 8-bit byte was established by Bemer as the fundamental unit of information, IBM discontinued its old 36-bit machines and brought out the 360 series. This HUGELY enlarged the market, but still with computer centers brainwashed by IBM. (DEC, with a much smaller segment of the market, also cut down to the 8-bit byte, leaving its PDP-10 and PDP-20 users high and dry.)

IBM CONSPIRACIES: There are those who thought that IBM was suppressing little computers. THEY DIDN'T HAVE A CLUE! The personal computer world was a complete shock to IBM. They believed computers had to be run by great squads supported by sales teams, even though DEC was already doing it differently.

IBM'S POWER IMAGE, around customer perception of reliability and conventionality, has been strangely recapitulated by Microsoft.

Chapter -16   Computer Sound and Music   (1947)

Summary. In 1947 they attach a loudspeaker to the ENIAC to hear its program counter-- helpful for debugging-- so computer sound and music begins. Academic composers makes an early start; digital music goes to the public when a highschool kid invents playing from music samples in the 1970s. 'We'll listen to music on computers', predicts a 1974 book; then Philips creates the CD and the special-purpose computer that plays it. But few realize it's a computer.

Now the world is a Babel of audio formats, and the music industry is trying to prevent their use. And thousands of guys are building 'prosumer' studios, hoping to be the next Wendy Carlos, but the problem is always distribution-- even with free downloads.

Computer sound and music cover a huge field: sound recording, sound playback, live performance sound synthesis and instruments, performance capture, layered composition, and distribution.

Electronic music begun in 1919: the Theremin (named after its creator), started a tradition of eerie spacey sounds.) Layered sound started with Les Paul and Mary Ford in the forties.

In 1947—the same time the LP came out-- they put a CRT on the ENIAC to hear its program counter-- helpful for debugging-- so computer sound and music began.

Academic composers made an early start: Leuning and Ussachevsky at Columbia, Milton Babbitt at Princeton (with RCA's sponsorship). But digital music hit the charts, and public awareness and public tinkering, when Harry Mendell, a highschool kid invented playing from music samples in the 1970s. (Harry's Melodian, superbly designed, was used by Stevie Wonder on his album "The Secret Life of Plants" in 1979. However, Harry rejected Wonder's backing for altruistic reasons.)*

```
                    *Harry Mendell, personal communication.
```

Philips, who had given us the audiocassette created the CD (actually the special-purpose computer that plays it)—defined in the Red Book standard, 1980. ('We'll listen to music on computers'-- *Computer Lib*, 1974)

Now the world is using hundreds of different audio formats in a Babel of incompatibilities and software installations, and the music industry is trying to prevent their use (see Intellectual Property, above).

And thousands of guys are building 'prosumer' studios, spending thousands on hardware and software, hoping to be the next Wendy Carlos. But the problem is always distribution... even with Lulu.

GEEKS BEARING GIFTS

Chapter -15 Computer Graphics in Two Dimensions (1950)

Summary. They put a CRT on the MIT Whirlwind computer in 1955 and so computer graphics begins. Immediately you could draw pictures, crudely at first, by program. But early computer graphics mostly uses character printout-- it's all that most guys have. (The Defense Department funds computer graphics, but that doesn't make graphics military. And that money went for a lot of game-playing, too.)

Then comes Sutherland's Sketchpad system for line drawing, which instead of mimicking one-sized paper can expand to the size of a football field; it expands a lot of minds.

As bits become cheaper and color displays arrive, paint systems make the pictures fancier. As with audio, a Babel of formats appears, and converting these formats becomes a huge issue. Then two brothers thousands of miles apart-- a movie special-effects guy and an academic-- program a graphics file converter that grows and grows and creates an enormous industry.

> **BREAKTHROUGH**: HOMOGENEOUS COOR-DINATES, discovered by Larry Roberts in the '60s, generalize and simplify rotation by adding an extra dimension (miscalled "the homogeneous coordinate"). Larry says this was just library research.* It also works for both 2D and 3D.*
> *Larry Roberts, personal communication.

> **BREAKTHROUGH**: THE ALPHA CHANNEL was invented/discovered by Alvy Ray Smith and Tom Duff in the 1970s, and compositing algebra for it.

GEEKS BEARING GIFTS   55

(This was similar to the BLIT breakthrough of Dan Ingalls; see Ch. 4.)

BREAKTHROUGH: THE BLIT (BLock Image Transfer, also BitBlt, pronounced. bitblit) was invented/discovered by Dan Ingalls, 1974. Blitting allows screenmapped images to be rapidly moved across one another. The Blit operations, algebraically combinable, are the technical foundation of modern bit-mapped screen interaction. It is presentationally neutral, adaptable to any style of presentation.

BREAKTHROUGH: FRACTALS. (See 3D.)

PACKAGE: PhotoShop, created by the Knoll brothers in their spare time, had no new techniques, but it puts a lot of methods together and brought a broad palette of 2D computer graphics to industry and the public.

There are two basic kinds of 2D computer graphics: the static kind that sit on your screen (and you can print on paper), and the kind that can be made interactive.

SKETCHPAD, THE DEFINING MOMENT. Ivan Sutherland's Sketchpad (1965), done on the experimental TX-2 graphics machine at Lincoln Labs, wows the world. It is a line-drawing program with a canvas that can be enlarged to a football field and can have many instances of the objects you draw. (It's an early OO program that later inspires Alan Kay.) Nothing has been as good since.

2D Graphics remained an academic pursuit until bit-mapped displays arrived (notably the 1973 Alto at Xerox PARC and, in the late seventies, graphics boards for dinky computers (such as the Video Dazzler, whose first program showed a winebottle endlessly pouring) and the graphics of the Apple II (which came in both high and lo-res versions).

The field quickly split into three separate pursuits: line drawing (ruled for a time by MacDraw; color (including grayscale); and photos. Many different formats appeared for color and photos, especially as the Macintosh took control (during the eighties) of the graphics arts market.

But as in all areas, warring formats get in the way of work and preservation-- .GIF created by CompuServe, .JPEG created by a committee, .PNG supposedly "lossless"-- and better ones we can't get.

THE BROTHERS. John and Thomas Knoll pursued seemingly different careers: John went into movies and became a special-effects honcho for Industrial Light and Magic, George Lucas' magic shop. Tom Knoll was working on visual perception research in the Midwest.

When the Macintosh came out, they were delighted by it, and (in their spare time) started creating translation programs for the different graphics formats. By and by they thought they might make a product out of it. They took a plug-in format from a prospective competitor, packaged all their converters and shopped around for the best distribution deal. Adobe took it and named the product Photoshop.

It turned out they had no competition. Photoshop has consistently controlled the industry ever since, clobbering a few challenger packages like Alvy Ray Smith's Altamira Composer (which let you pop pieces of pictures together with perfect edges—in Photoshop that takes much training and many stages) and Live Picture, which worked with proxy representations and rendered later. It was buggy, but had great fans--

Photoshop is a nice tool, and it does the job well, but it pales in comparison to what a skilled graphic artist could do with Live Picture. And Live Picture could easily and responsively work with a 200 Megabyte graphic image - even several of them, working with them as a composite, on a Mac 7500/120 with 32 megabytes of memory.
– Michael D. Crawford

INTERACTIVE 2D. Today, on the Web, there are numerous formats for interactive 2D—starting, for example, with picture maps that allow clicking of various parts of the picture (server side image maps, client side image maps). Trying to keep track of Web formats is like trying to keep track of celebrities—they come and go, with in general little consequence.

A key exception is Flash.

FLASH. Adobe Flash rules in interaction today. We need to distinguish between what it can do, its data structure, and its grotesque programmer's interface.

> **What Flash can do.** Flash is essentially a complete platform—a complete program package with all forms of graphics, interaction and communication. In a Flash package (.swf file) you can have movies, audio, rich programs of any complexity, and connection to various servers.
>
> The niftiest example of Flash programming is the "Flash Wireframe Skeleton"§, which is a beautiful example of interaction, simulation programming, medical illustration, and superbly designed interaction. [We would appreciate knowing who the author is.]
>
> Unlike any other program, Flash allows you to zoom on fonts without jerky movement, which conventional font methods give you as the font size increases and decreases.

The Flash Data Structure. Flash has two data structures, the working data structure and the output data structure (.swf). After some political wrangles, Adobe has opened up the Flash data internals to some degree and people are creating alternative methods of building Flash presentations and programs.

The Flash programmer's interface evolved from the earlier Director interface which had a parallel timeline like music notation. This was used to make multilayer animation clips. In addition, it contains Javascript (more properly, ECMAscript), for full programming capability and the manipulation of these pieces. The Flash programmer's system is very expensive and hard to learn, but very powerful.

FLASH HISTORY. Flash began as "SmartSketch" created by Jonathan Gay in 1993. It was then adapted for the Web as FutureSplash Animator, which was sold to MacroMedia. The interface was strongly influenced by Director.

Flash animations can be shown everywhere except the Iphone (some say because of control issues).

Chapter -14 Computer Games, 1951

Summary. Back in the '50s, computer games are a furtive amusement when you sneak time on the lab machine. No one imagines the immensity of the industry to come, whose revenue now outstrips Hollywood.

Early text games like Hunt The Wumpus and Zork became MUDs and MOOs and WOOs. A company called Atari puts out a minimalist game called Pong with minimalist directions (HIT BALL BACK FOR HIGH SCORE). From there it's only a few years to the spectacular explosion of Pac-Man, 1981-- with movie-size revenues-- and that's before networks or realistic graphics.

First-person shooters start with 'Star Trek' in the mid-seventies and now explode visually in blood and phlegm. Multi-player role games, starting with Dungeons and Dragons (no computers), have become vast industries. Today's Serious Gamer (oxymoron) is a white guy with no girlfriend and a computer costing ten grand or more. Go figure.

Now the computer game industry is supposedly bigger than Hollywood. The University of California at Santa Cruz creates a department of computer games and their enrollment shoots instantly past computer science.

The first computer game was in a patent application in 1948. But possibly the first working computer game was Spacewar! on a PDP-1 at MIT (1961-- Martin Graetz, Alan Kotok, Steve Russell).

ARCADE GAMES. The first coin-operated game was The Galaxy Game, of which one was built, and it ran at Tressider Hall at Stanford in 1971, a few months before the better-known Computer Space by Nolan Bushnell and Ted Dabney. Bushnell and Dabney realized that was too complicated and created the extremely simple game called Pong, which was a huge hit. (Documentation consisted entirely of the instruction: HIT BALL BACK FOR HIGH SCORE.)

By the mid-seventies the coin-op games, and the video arcades they spawn, are huge business. Smash successes include Space Invaders and Pac-Man. (The formula is always the same: you will die soon, but the more skillful you become, the longer you can postpone it. Kind of like real life.)

COMPUTER GAMES. Games come on the first computers, including Breakout (son of Pong, programmed by Jobs'n'Woz) and Star Trek (basically the massacre of Klingons, by galactic sector). Now Windows comes with standard solitaire, chewing gum for the mind.

HAND-HELD GAMES. In the seventies, hand-held digital games appeared. In 1989, Nintendo releases the GameBoy, which goes on to sell over a hundred million units world-wide.

BIG-IRON GAME CONSOLES. Today there are two big game consoles: the PlayStation from Sony (whose 3D software uses OpenGL) and the Xbox from Microsoft (whose 3D software uses DirectX). Both of them are powerful general-purpose computers underneath, but the manufacturers deliberately prevent their use as computers. Besides the general-purpose architecture, however, they have remarkable circuitry for such special graphic functions as smoke generation.

These are built for the Serious Gamer (oxymoron?), typically a bachelor in his 20s or 30s who spends tens of thousands of dollars on this addiction.

A surprising new hit, however, is the Wii from Nintendo, which is based on a simpler model of play: instead of multilevel games that take weeks to get into, the Wii is for friends at a party who want a zero-learning-time way of having fun together. And the paddles it comes with—which sense position and acceleration-- can be used in a surprising variety of ways.

ROLE-PLAYING GAMES, in life and on various machines. Role-playing games have existed since time immemorial—remember Cowboys and Indians?—but Gary Gygax made it an industry with his classic "Dungeons and Dragons" (1974) where a Dungeonmaster ruled an imaginary kingdom that was shared through story-telling and dice rolling; the Dungeonmaster could always tilt the odds to keep the game even, and the shared visualization through storytelling was a central part of it. With computerization came a crucial change: no longer was there a dungeonmaster or a shared story; you saw it on the screen and the odds were no longer manipulated. Such games were different. But they've caught on very, very big. You can play them alone, with friends at home, or on line with people you never see--

MASSIVE MULTIPLAYER ON-LINE ROLE GAMES (MMPORGs) are a huge industry (half a billion dollars revenue in 2005). The first MMPORG was *Mazewar* (1973, created by Steve Colley at NASA). The first one with real graphics was *Neverwinter Nights* (1991, AOL). *Final Fantasy* has gone through many successive versions. *World of Warcraft* carries on. Sony's *Everquest* remains a top grosser.

LEVELS, POWERS, QUESTS, MONSTERS AND LOOT: Typically the MMPORG player ascends through levels of power and strength, acquiring loot along the way, joining in Quests with other players. Monsters are encountered and vanquished, loot is acquired. From a revenue point of view, it is essential that the player be teased into wasting as much time as possible ascending through various levels of ability and power. ("Levelling services" exist, where you pay people in faroff lands to run your character for many hours to get more powers you don't have time and patience for.)

Chapter -13 Disk Drive Wars   (1956)

Summary.   IBM creates the RAMAC, a computer with a disk drive, in 1955. This leads to the issue of how to organize information on disks. Guys with different views create different kinds of filing and naming conventions.

The program and tables required for each disk idea are called a filesystem. The main filesystems right now are FAT (Windows, left over from Tim Patterson's Quick and Dirty Operating System); NTFS, better than FAT, created for Windows; HFS, the Macintosh filesystem, which has gotten good; and Ext2, the main filesystem for Gnu/Linux. There are many more. (The three-letter extension often used for file types is also left over from QDOS All the FAT fileystems have it inside.)

Different filesystems allow different alphabets and alphabetical orders. This makes it hard to keep your files lined up in a given sequence, especially if you use different computers or have drives with more than one filesystem.

There are few difference among filesystems; most closely follow the Unix model. And alas, one of the few innovators in filesystem design is now in prison for murder.

DISK FILE PROBLEMS OF ORDINARY PEOPLE
The concept of a file evolved only gradually to a standard method, with Unix in 1970. To the people privileged to use Unix then, it was a great privilege.

But now, for the public, things have changed. Today's rigidly hierarchical filesystems have deep consequences for users' lives.

EVERYBODY'S PROBLEMS WITH FILESYSTEMS.
So many of the problems people have with computers are about--
- how to fit their content into hierarchies and filenames
- how to save complex data (Web saves are particularly bad)
- things that criss-cross and overlap and interpenetrate like the real concerns of our documents and lives

Ordinary people have trouble figuring out where to put things—
- with multiple uses
- with evolving concepts
- projects that split and join
- having to move and rename them, breaking connections

THE BACKUP PROBLEM. Typically people back up a lump of hierarchical data by putting it in another lump of hierarchical data, and that runs out of namespace.

These problems are treated by the technical community as simply the rules of the cosmos. But no one seems to know that they could be different.

PECULIARITIES OF DISK SYSTEMS
File and metadata. A file consists of a payload and metadata—a name and other information that are carried along with it. These are usually the owner, permissions for the file's use, date created, and date last modified. All these are from Unix.

The Inode table. Unix created a special method for keeping track of files and directories: a single table in which each file and directory is listed. Because the table has a fixed width (now usually 512 characters), the names of a file and all the directories above it—the full pathname-- must not exceed this length. The problems of such a method are obvious.

PROBLEMS OF THE STANDARD (UNIX) FILE MODEL. Nearly all filesystems today are based on the Unix model, in their file model, in their full hierarchy, and in manipulation by an inode table.

• **Hierarchy**. You have to map everything into hierarchical structure, even though they have multiple uses. Shortcuts are a small compensation.

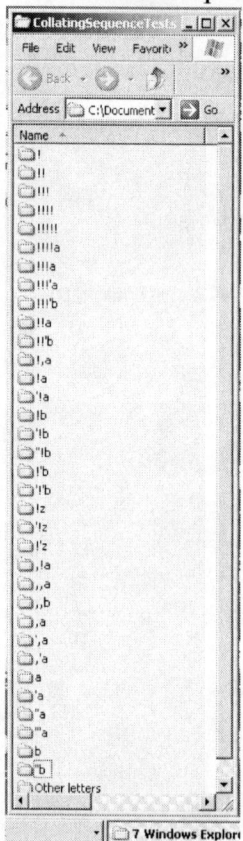

• **Shortcuts** (called aliases on the Macintosh, links under Unix). The standard model allows only one-way shortcuts that do not follow the files when moved or renamed, and total pathname length limited by the Inode table.

• **Metadata**: you can't see it and you can't create your own metadata types. Because of this, you have to cram a great deal of information into the filename itself—metadata that has to be visible. This makes many filenames horribly unreadable.

• **The inode table** (invisible). The fixed width of the Inode table creates problems for backup and even files that become lost.

Beware: Keeping things in 'My Documents' and 'Desktop' gives them very long pathnames-- this has drastic consequences for keeping Web pages, for example

FILESYSTEMS AND PARTITIONS. Different people with slightly different ideas have created different ways of storing on disk; these are called filesystems. Each requires its own particular program and tables, besides the drive itself. A filesystem consists of the contents of a disk, with the data that holds its structure, and the program that reads it and writes it. (Or perhaps only reads it.) Every drive, or partition, requires a filesystem.

The commands of the filesystem are principally "read" and "write", but with many helping functions the user doesn't see, like "flush" (complete operations and empty buffers). This leads to interesting thoughts about extending filesystem functions, like Hans Reiser (below).

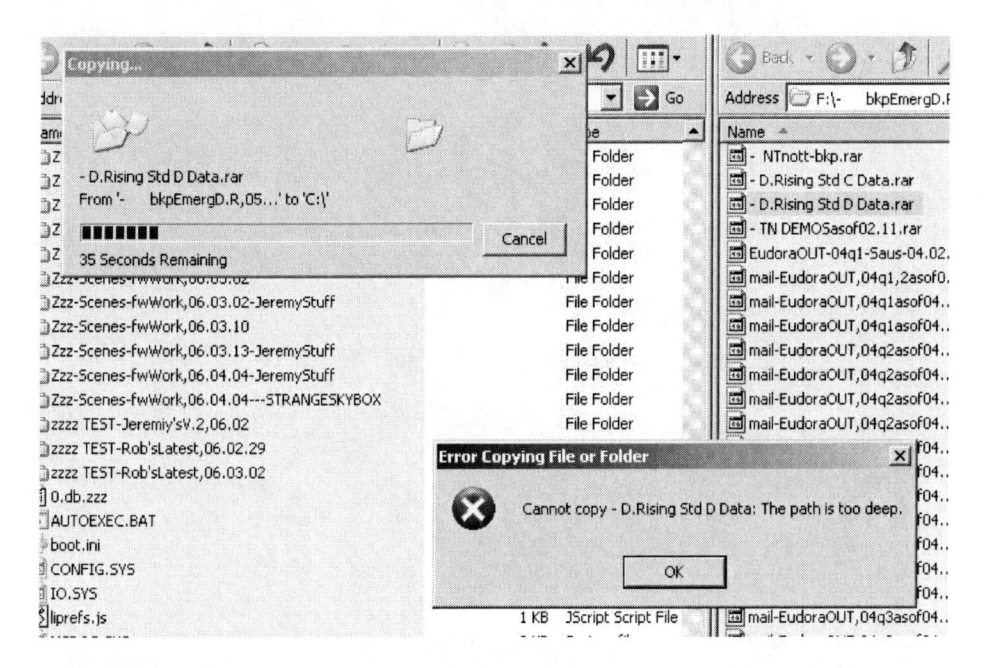

USING DIFFERENT FILESYSTEMS
In principle you could use any filesystem under any operating system, IF you can get a reliable program to read and write it.

BUT: WINDOWS READING MAC, AND VICE VERSA
Example: Macintosh OS X will read (but not write) Windows NTFS drives. You can buy a program to write them from Paragon Software (G4 and Intel Macs only). Windows will not read or write Macintosh HFS drives, but you can buy a program called MacDrive7 to read and write them.

(These incompatibilities derive not from any technical restrictions, but from the residual pettiness between Jobs and Gates and the calculated incompatibilities they maintain between their two systems.)

A LEVER FOR CHANGE? It has been pointed out that completely different filesystems could be created, doing special things (such as database) inside the file mechanism. (An innovator in filesystem design, Hans Reiser, was planning to put database features into the filesystem itself; see below.)

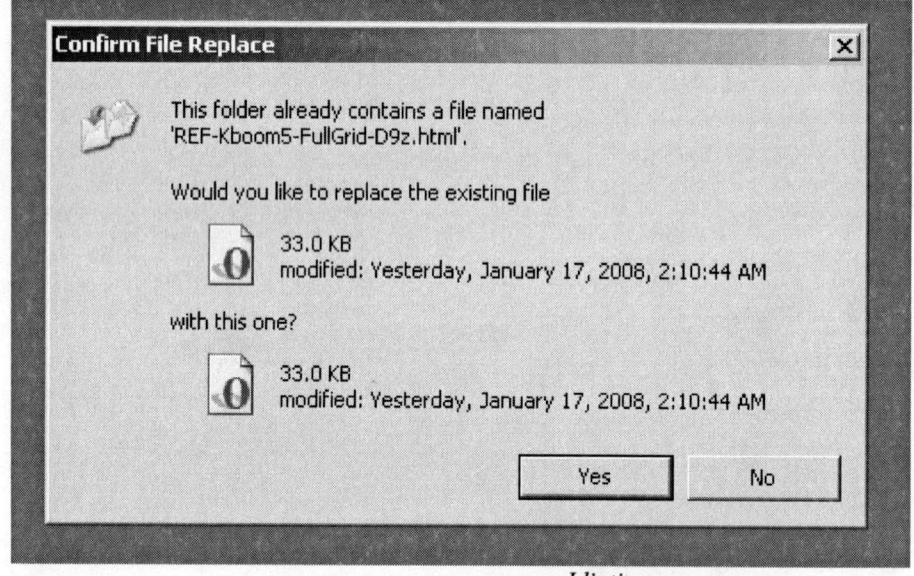

Idiotic error message.
The system is perfectly capable
Of recognizing the identity of the two files
and not bothering you about it.

Different alphabetical orders: "filesystem localization". Different filesystems allow different alphabetical orders, making it hard to keep your files lined up the same way on different machines. But part of this has to do with the way you customize a drive when you format it. For instance, if you format a drive with an NTFS filesystem under Windows, it will take information on where you are and make decisions about how the bytes will be interpreted—what they will look like and what order they will sort in. They don't tell you this, of course.

LITTLE-KNOWN FACT: Reiser's innovation and imprisonment. One of the few innovators in filesystem design is now in prison for murder. Hans Reiser created his filesystem, ReiserFS, with the intent of creating a whole new way of incorporating database within the filesystem itself.* Working in Russia where programmers were inexpensive, he met his Russian wife and moved to Berkeley. After her disappearance, he was tried for murder—without a corpus delicti. But now he has confessed, and ReiserFS is on hold for a long time.

*Andrew Pam, personal communication.

Chapter -12 Engelbart's NLS (1958)

Summary. The story in brief: A soft-spoken and lovable farm boy, nicknamed in the navy "EagleBeak" for his fierce profile, Engelbart sets out to solve the world's hardest problems with superpowerful collaboration tools. It is Doug Engelbart who first puts document work on screens and invents multiple windows on a screen, links among texts, shared work on screens, and much more-- including the mouse (which he disdains as a small matter).

Engelbart's fabulous prototype NLS (oN-Line System), demonstrated at the Fall Joint Computer Conference in 1968, wows the computer world.

But that world's attention shifts. Engelbart's ideas are too radical and his interface too daunting, and in the next decade the computer world goes for fonts on paper instead of collaboration on screens. Doug's work is overlooked by acclamation. Worse, his vision of accelerating collaborative power is forgotten or considered impossible. Doug's vision, like Tesla's, is too sweeping for mortals. But some believe the time for Engelbart's ideas will come again.

People remember Doug Engelbart for inventing the mouse, which is ridiculous. Compared to his other work the mouse was inconsequential, as he himself insists. "That's just something we did on the weekend," he says. His work is celebrated but not appreciated for its full vision.

It was Doug Engelbart who came up with the idea of documents on a computer screen and ways we could work on them together. As far as he's concerned, that's still not working right. And what he wants people to see is his overall vision of a world of accelerating team creativity-- tackling the hardest problems of resources, pollution, population, crime, disarmament, global warming-- and finding the solutions through deep collaboration.

Doug Engelbart was always saintly. As a boy in rural Oregon, he fainted when he was asked to speak in church.* As a sailor in the Pacific in WWII, he read Bush's famous article and imagined a new world of information sharing.

*Doug Enbelbart, personal communication.

Other people work on local problems and projects, taking small steps, but Engelbart always thought big. Why worry about little problems when it's the big ones that we must face? This means collaborating on a scale and with a clarity and scope that has never existed before.

After the Navy he got a Ph.D. in electrical engineering, but his mind was on human intellect and collaboration. "How can I *really* make a difference?" he asked himself. Then it dawned on him (1958) that reading, writing and sharing on computer screen could provide the answer to mankind's greatest problems—which begin with the small problems of information handling and presentation.

He assembled a team at Stanford University with sponsorship from ARPA and particularly Bob Taylor. Someone else was giving the presentation to Taylor, but Doug was quietly masterminding the proceedings, and Taylor said, "I want to sponsor *him!*"* (People from those days who are around him still include Bill English, Bill Duvall, Ann Duvall, Jeff Rulifson.)

*Doug Engelbart, personal communication.

These were the glory days of NLS. With that funding, Doug and his group created their text system of unprecedented power (unequalled even today). It allowed simultaneous text work by people in different locations, including annotation and linkage. It was a collaborative system such as the world had never seen.

The world saw it in fall of 1968—a select few who will never forget. This was Doug's legendary Great Demo. It should not have worked. There were too many things to wrong. And it all worked perfectly. The demo in 1968, from the convention hall in San Francisco to the relay truck on Skyline Highway to Jeff Rulifson back at the lab at SRI, back to the convention hall and the unthinkable Eidophor projector and Doug's understated explanations into the mike—all, all went flawlessly.

The world has not been the same since.

But Doug's path seemed too complicated. His interface language did not have ready appeal. The PUI took over (see Chapter 3).

Doug believes that with the right tools, human capability can accelerate geometrically. Few others can quite see that; his vision of accelerating collaborative power has been forgotten or considered impossible. Doug's vision, like Tesla's, is too sweeping for mortals. (He works on, aided especially by his daughter Christina and his clever long-time secretary, Mary Coppernoll.)

But visionaries always have a hard time, even when everyone pays them homage. Perhaps the next generation will listen, and the time for Engelbart's ideas will come again.

CONNECTIONS. Deep interconnection was one of Doug's greatest contributions. Doug's system allowed extensive connections--
- a user could link to, and annotate, portions within a document.
- a 'plex' of connections could gather together a number of different entities.

These facilities are missing from software even today.

Chapter -11 Xanadu (1960)

Summary. A young filmmaker-intellectual and friends, envisioning the total replacement of paper by the computer screen, contrive a radical system of side-by-side documents with visible connection, and sales methods for a new world-wide electronic publishing industry.

Xanadu is not (as often supposed) a bungled attempt to create the World Wide Web; it is a sweeping design for text, audio and video in a uniform structure that can be shown many different ways (**WYSIWYNC**); but always with the options of side-by-side intercomparison and visible re-use. Instead of a single visualization (as with Acrobat or Microsoft Word), new programmable visions of any kind are welcome; but the canonical vision is side-by-side parallel strips with visible connections.

Rather than imitating the past (like paper and movies that can only be sequential), Xanadu is a radical generalization of media, work systems, organizing methods and copyright-- to do everything previously possible with text and movies, and much more that still is not.

For half a century the project expands and contracts, boggled by opposing computer traditions, premature optimization, culture clashes and infighting.

Xanadu is far simpler than the Web, but utterly incompatible because of the Web's iron browser standard, which forbids all Xanadu methods and views. "We fight on", say Xanadu diehards.

A guy recently out of college, with a film and some original work already behind him, came to the wild surmise in 1960 that paper will be replaced by the computer screen, even though at that time there were no computer screens in civilian hands. He set out to design a whole system of literature to replace all systems of writing and publication. (He wanted to make movies, but instead took a couple of years out to design more generalized movies and documents; as with many who entered the field early, those couple of years became half a century.) The Xanadu project has had many participants (fifty to a hundred, depending on how you count) and locations in various states and countries.

FUNDAMENTAL ISSUES. A complete literature meant taking into account the way writing is done, the many uses and re-uses of content, the problem of versioning (and especially distributing updates), and finally a system of commerce and personal ownership comparable to owning books; this is deeply important to scholars and people in general.

> THE BASIC XANADU DATA STRUCTURE IS SO SIMPLE—
> A collage of content with overlays, sent out as a list.

It took two decades to get the data structure right; but unfortunately the project got hung up on keeping track of re-use among millions of documents. (Note that this was before the Internet.) Brilliant mathematical work was done on this problem by a number of people, but neither of two big implementations was finished due to infighting. The current endeavor is client-based and much simpler.

STABILIZED CONTENT ADDRESSES. We need to be able to refer to the same content bytes by the same addresses. For example, Lincoln's words "Fourscore and seven years ago" ideally have the same permaddress everywhre they appear, i.e.
 ['Gettysburg Address' ID] 0-2

This is far from current practice, but doable in two ways: (1) giving permaddresses to cooperative systems which are playing the game; (2) handling random content from the net by giving it time-and-address IDs.

TWO-WAY LINKS. A Xanadu two-way link can be published by itself. When you click on it, it brings up the original content at both ends. When you click on the two-way link as part of a particular document collage, it connects to whatever content in that document it connects to.

A DIFFERENT DOCUMENT. The traditional computer document is an iron box of characters in sequence, with no tracking of their origins. This is true of textfiles, Microsoft Word, Adobe Acrobat and Web pages. (The last three all have markup mangled into their content.) The Xanadu document is a collage assembled by the user's client program, then sandwiched with a selection of links, markup and overlays.
- Since every portion in the collage knows its original address, each original context is accessible
- Links can overlap in any number and have any number of types
- Rights management: the publisher allows re-use in any new context, since the original context is always accessible and each downloader purchases each portion. The structure for payment, which many have decried as some kind of attack on freedom, is intended to loosen the rigidity of the content industries (who will not give up copyright) while providing a win-win for all sides, allowing frictionless re-use, anthologies and mashup.

WYSIWYNC. The data structure is extremely simple but can be seen in many ways (WYSIWYNC—What You See Is What You Never Could (Before)). Instead of a single locked visualization (as with Word, Acrobat and the Web), new programmable visions of any kind are welcome; but the canonical vision is side-by-side connected strips—an unlimited fabric of strips and streams visibly connected by links and identities of content. This minimalist design intrinsically solves many problems of work, connection and versioning.

GEEKS BEARING GIFTS

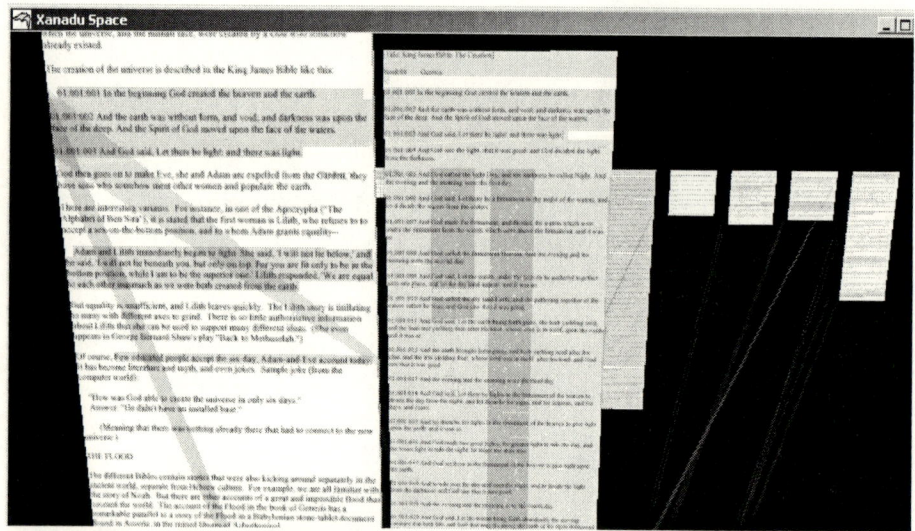

XANADU AND THE WEB. Xanadu and the World Wide Web are totally different and incompatible. The Web has one-way links and a fixed rectangular visualization based on the strictly-enforced rules of the browser. The browser will not composite or intercompare side by side.

Xanadu alumni consider the Web illicit and broken, exactly what they were trying to prevent— for having only one-way links, for conflating a document with a place, for locking it to one view, for having no way to maintain identifiable content from other sources, for having no means of visible connection to points within a document, for imposing hierarchy in a variety of ways.

The Xanadu data structure is far simpler than HTML, but utterly different. Primary content is never changed; it is assemblies of content that change. The Xanadu document is an assembly of content pieces with overlays, distributed indirectly as a list of content pieces and overlays to be sent for, assembled and presented.

Blogs, wikis and tagging were always built into the data structure-- not as separate features but intrinsic to the design, with only client tweaks needed to show them.

GEEKS BEARING GIFTS 75

The project was stalled by organizational politics, premature optimization, and simply the problem of explaining. Diehards go on with the project, sure of its depth and final success.

> **TRANSCLUSION:** the same content knowably in more than one place, by whatever method. Like Google snips.

RELATED WORK.
- Vannevar Bush's proposed "memex" (1945§) was designed with both links and transclusions, like Xanadu and unlike the Web.
- Wikipedia is built of transclusions, exactly like the basic Xanadu substratum, but without overlays. (see: "Wikipedia:Transclusion"§)
- Bill Duvall, an alumnus of NLS and PARC, tried implementing Engelbart'NLS a different way as an experiment. Instead of moving the text around, as the original NLS (and other systems) do, he tried editing it by changing pointers to fixed text (always the Xanadu method) and found this method faster and more efficient.*

*Bill Duvall, personal communication.
- Wendy Hall's Microcosm system, from the University of Southampton, was strongly influenced by Xanadu and had two-way links. Microcosm evolved through a number of different structures and business problems, but there remains a link server for two-way links ("Auld Linky").
- Jason Rohrer's TokenWord§ system is explicitly a working miniature version of Xanadu, including royalty publication.
- Today's cluttered web pages often bring in content from many different sources, as in the Xanadu model, but as separate graphical units to be distributed around the page. The browser cannot assemble consecutive text or video from separately-arriving portions, as in the Xanadu model.
- Google is now preparing to sell snippets of content, as Xanadu has always advocated; could work with Xanadu client programs.

Xanadu is about connections, content uses,
and their unlimited visualization
in parallel;
the Web is about fonts, hierarchy
and outward links only.

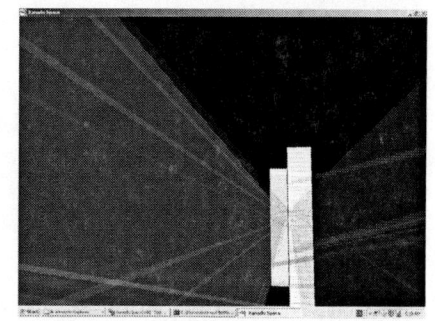

76 GEEKS BEARING GIFTS

Chapter -10 Computer Graphics in Three Dimensions   (1960)

Summary.   Computer 3D is with us everywhere today-- realistic fake movies, photographs mixed with fantasy elements, gaming and Second Life. But it took decades to get here, but the goal is realism. There are many techniques for presenting it and representing it.   3D games optimize one way, 3D movies another. And anyone can do it.

Computer 3D is with us everywhere today-- realistic fake movies, photographs mixed with fantasy elements, gaming and Second Life. But it took decades to get here.

There are many techniques for presenting it-- the fastest way, used by gamers, is OpenGL (or the Microsoft competitor, DirectX); the slowest is ray-tracing, the ultimate fine-grain method, looking down a virtual soda straw one pixel at a time; the middle way is RenderMan, which uses tricks and heuristics to present huge scenes in seeming detail without ray tracing.

There are many 3D representations. OpenGL (a legacy from Silicon Graphics) uses triangles stitched in 3D and painted with pictures (oddly called textures).   But there are also spline meshes, constructive solid geometry, metaballs (not meatballs, especially suited to fantastic writhing undersea shapes). And then there's building a creature up from moving bones (inverse kinematics), pioneered by Dennis Muren and the ILM team for "Jurassic Park".

BEING THERE.   When interactive 3D arrives, some want to colonize it as "virtual reality" (a term invented by a French theatrical director). But the moneymakers wonder, how to sell real estate in it? That's what Second Life has figured out. (See "Web 2.0".)

3D GAMES are now high voltage (see Games)-- on line, or on today's superboxes (Playstation and Xbox).

3D MOVIES. In the '60s and '70s people rolled their own 3D movie-making systems. Now lots are available, from zero up to stratospheric prices. (See Movies.) Talk continues of three-dimensional viewing systems without glasses, but the only proposed methods are absurdly expensive.

> **BREAKTHROUGH**: Larry Roberts' 3D method, generalizing and simplifying rotation by adding an extra dimension ("homogeneous coordinates"). Larry says this was 'just library research'; he found it in the '60s, but it was worked out in theory in the 19th Century*. It also works for 2D.
> *Larry Roberts, personal communication.

> **BREAKTHROUGH:** ALPHA CHANNEL (see 2D).

> **BREAKTHROUGH**: FRACTALS (self-similar recursive patterns), the lifetime work of mathematician Benoit Mandelbrot, allow the creation of remarkably realistic structures by very simple recursive programming. Interesting in 2D, luscious in 3D. Used by various landscape programs, as well as in movies.

> **BREAKTHROUGH**: Gouraud Shading, discovered by a computer-science student, is a breakthrough in fast graphical presentation. Gouraud discovered that a sculpture of triangles can be made to look solid and

curvy by simple interpolation— a completely nonintuitive discovery.

PACKAGE: OpenGL, the fast system derived from Gouraud shading, is a set of routines to be embedded in C and C++ programs.

Computer 3D— seeming photographs, simulated objects, realistic scenes with depth-- are with us everywhere today. The question is, what *isn't* fake? Fake movies are realistic, photographs in ads are now scrambled with fantasy elements. 3D games take up some people's lives, as does a commercial world called Second Life. But it took decades to get here.

In the 3D work of the '60s, first they drew boxes and figured which lines would be hidden. Then they realized you didn't have to follow lines to make a picture: you could make photograph-like pictures in completely different ways. Ray tracing (very slow) and Gouraud shading (very fast but inaccurate) became opposite lines of development. This means that if you want to play games, you want fast response, and if you want to render movies you want slow precise output.

REPRESENTATION. There are many 3D representations. OpenGL uses triangles stitched in 3D and painted with pictures (oddly called textures). But there are also spline meshes, constructive solid geometry, metaballs (not meatballs)-- especially suited to fantastic writhing undersea shapes. And then there's building a creature up from moving bones (inverse kinematics), pioneered by Dennis Muren and the ILM team for "Jurassic Park".

PRESENTATION METHODS. There are faster and faster 3D graphic machines (see below), but the software methods are crucial--
Fast presentation software. The fastest way, used by gamers, is triangular-stitching of shapes and covering them with pictures (textures). The two main systems are OpenGL (or the Microsoft competitor, DirectX); these are descended from the Gouraud method of the 1960s.

Slow presentation software. Ray-tracing, the ultimate fine-grain method, looks down a virtual soda straw one pixel at a time. This is for extremely accurate visualization.

Middle-way software. the middle way is RenderMan, created by Pixar and made available as an open standard (but they sell the software). It uses tricks and heuristics to build huge scenes in unlimited-seeming detail without ray tracing. You'll see RenderMan screen credits on such films as Wall-E, whose detailed and intricate scenes were managed and presented by RenderMan software.

3D GAMES are now high voltage (see Games)-- on line, or on today's superboxes (Sony Playstation and Microsoft Xbox).

BEING THERE. What lies beyond gaming? Well, living, sort of. When interactive 3D loomed, some wanted to colonize it, projecting themselves into this new space. They call interactive 3D "virtual reality" (a term invented by a French theatrical director, Antonin Artaud, in the 1930s). As popularized today, VR seems to mean artificial, literal 3D—so if something is a hundred virtual feet away in the space, you've got to go a hundred virtual feet to get there. Interactive idealists Jaron Lanier, Scott Fisher and Brenda Laurel have popularized this notion. However, less idealistic types have wondered, how to sell real estate in it? That's what Second Life has figured out: you buy lots and islands in their world with LindenDollars, which convert to and from real money. (See "Web 2.0".)

FAST MACHINES. Of course, this all has to be carried out in hardware, the faster the better. Wonderful fast machines from the late lamented Silicon Graphics were superseded by generic machines (i.e., IBM PCs) with fast graphic engines, (usually add-in boards). Gamers demand super performance. This typically falls out to regular users a few years later, so that most computer users now have graphics which were unthinkable when personal computers began. There are of course the two gaming supermachines, PlayStation (Sony) and Xbox (Microsoft), carefully controlled by their manufacturers. While these can be viewed as very powerful general-purpose computers, anything with smoke-generator pipelines is a little more than general purpose.

GRAPHICS BOARDS, AND THEIR AVAILABILITY FOR OTHER PURPOSES. With astonishing swiftness, different new architectures for graphics boards come and go, in a six-month product cycle. Today's PC graphics boards outperform the computer itself, which is locked into its functions. The graphics boards' strange configurations are designed for high-speed pipelining of graphics data, but recently they have been extended for general use by those who know how to mess with it. A new field is developing to use this super side-power, with the terrible acronym GPGPU, for General Purpose Computing on Graphics Processing Units. It will probably get a better name.

MOVIES OF 3D SCENES, EVERYWHERE. In the '60s and '70s people rolled their own 3D systems. Now lots of such systems are available, from zero up to stratospheric prices. (See Movies.)

Chapter -9 The ARPANET Gets the Message Across   (1962)

Summary. A jovial psychologist proposes communication amongst everybody by computer. The Defense Department (ARPA division) thinks it's a good idea.

Meanwhile a Rand Corporation engineer, grimly worried about nuclear war, invents packet switching, in hopes of keeping a thermonuclear exchange from escalating to doomsday. Though opposed by telephone veterans, it works. It triumphs over telephone traditions and networking methods developed by IBM and ISO. The Pentagon funds it and it barely works, but not all the information arrives across the network. A Frenchman says, Why not have the endpoints take care of completing the exchange? The result is TCP/IP, a new way to push-pull information across a tangle of connections. It barely works, and connects a lot of researchers on their separate networks across a big supernetwork that barely works.

First it's called the ARPAnet, run with the flavor of military culture. But the military-- who inspired it in the first place-- sees that it's totally insecure and gives it to the public. It still barely works. (It's still totally insecure, but we now call it the Internet. See Chapter 12.)

THE STORY IN BRIEF. Many essayists, including H.G. Wells and Vannevar Bush, imagined communication networks of writings. But it took off when an amiable psychologist called Lick (J.C.R. Licklider) proposed it seriously within the government funding community.

Anywhere else this would have gotten lost. But it happened that Lick was at the cutting edge, a small important agency with a loose mandate-- the Defense Department's ARPA/IPT (Advanced Researched Projects Agency, Information Processing Technology section). The idea was seized by Bob Taylor and others.

They found an ingenious and unlikely method proposed by a very worried engineer, Paul Baran, at the Rand Corporation. (Also invented by a Brit, in parallel—a very smart guy who'd found a bug in Turing's code.)

Like many others in the 1950s defense establishment (and on the other side as well), Baran was extremely concerned about the possibility of accidental nuclear war, and rightly so. The issue he seized was a grim one: in the event of one or a few nuclear bombs going off, how to maintain communication so retaliation could be certain; or better, so the next ones could be stopped (whether by diplomacy or, however unthinkable, surrender). The main thing was for the government to keep communications up and not go helpless.

But what if the phones were out? What if radio lines (and there were many) were out, in some strange pattern? How could word get through?

Here was Baran's idea. Instead of communicating across a fixed line, which required in those days specific radio or dot-dash-type signals, communicate in a series of digital packets, and send them in all directions.

> BARAN: We chose not to classify this work and also chose not to patent the work. We felt that it properly belonged in the public domain. Not only would the US be safer with a survivable command and control system, the US would be even safer if the USSR also had a survivable command and control system as well! There was never any desire for

--transcript of "Oral history interview with Paul Baran"
by Judy E. O'Neill, Babbage Institute §.

'The most important event of the twentieth century is one that didn't happen.'
Thomas Schelling on nuclear war, in his Nobel speech.

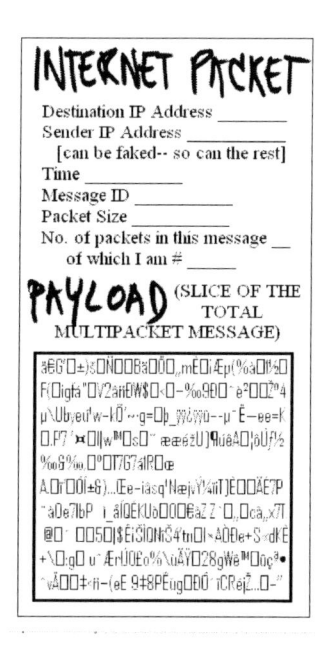

INTERNET PACKET

Destination IP Address _____
Sender IP Address _____
  [can be faked-- so can the rest]
Time _____
Message ID _____
Packet Size _____
No. of packets in this message ___
  of which I am # _____

PAYLOAD (SLICE OF THE TOTAL MULTIPACKET MESSAGE)

```
aŝG˜⊡±)š⊡N⊡⊡Ḃa⊡Ö⊡„mË⊡ìÆp(%ȧ⊡ṫ⁵⊡
Fï⊡igta"⊡V2añËW$⊡‹⊡‑‰9Ḃ⊡·é²⊡⊡ẑ⁰4
µ\Ửb̦ȩü'w‑l⊡'…g=⊡p̦_₁₉₃⟨⟩ü‑‑µ¨Ë‑ėė=k
⊡.Ṗ7´⋈⊡‖₁w⁽ᵐ⊡s⊡¨ææéźU]9uȧÅ⊡}öÜ̦ʲ½
‰ĝ‰·⊡°⊡T7Ĝ74lṖ⊡œ
A.⊡r⊡⊡l±6̦)…[Ëe‑iȧsqʼNæjıY⁴ãïT]Ë⊡⊡ÅËṖ
¨a⊡e7bP⌐ı⎯ȧl⊡EKUb⊡⊡⊡ȧZZ¨⊡_⊡cȧ˛ˌx⊡T|
@⊡¨⊡⊡5⊡|$ËíȜl⊡Nĵ5̧4ʼtn⊡l‑A⊡Ḃe+S¨dłË
+\⊡;g⊡ u¨ÆrÜlÖ£o⁰⁄₀\üÃỸ⊡28gWė⁽ᵐ⊡ö¢⁹•
¨vÅ⊡⊡‡¨n̄‑(eË·9‡8PËügṘ⊡Ḃ⊡¨iCRêȷ̧2̦‥⊡‑ʼ
```

83

Packet switching, as Baran planned it, would involve blocks of data, each sent toward a specific destination address. Each block would be sent digitally into a new kind of network. Each block would say at the beginning where it was bound, and a packet switch (now called a router) would whack each block in the right direction toward the address it carried. (Baran called them blocks; the next guy to invent the method called them packets.)

AT&T, which was then the phone monopoly, didn't want to hear about it, and the old-time phone engineers would talk down to Baran as if he were a child. But Baran persisted. ('It takes thirty to sixty briefings to get an idea across', he now says laconically.)

So administrators at ARPA pushed the project—Bob Taylor, Larry Roberts, Ivan Sutherland—to create a shared network for scientists and researchers. The emphasis was no longer on preventing nuclear war—building a secure system was for another branch of Defense, and they were doing a first try in an unknown area.

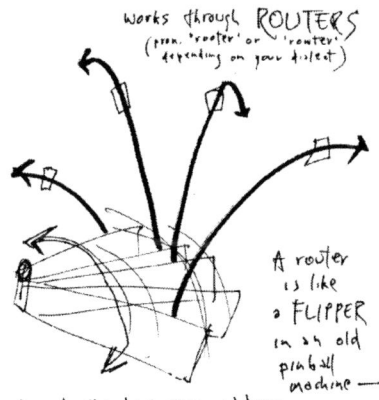

INTERNET PROTOCOL (IP) is the ARPANET's specific version of packet-switching from point to point. (It can branch to find a successful route, as Baran intended, but usually does not.)

ROUTERS. The idea of having a separate machine for packet

PACKET SWITCHING

Works through ROUTERS
(pron. 'rooter' or 'rowter' depending on your dialect)

A router is like a FLIPPER in an old pinball machine — it reads the destination address of each packet, then whacks it further in that direction (selecting a particular wire), millions of times per second.

switching was proposed by Wes Clark (creator of the original DEC modules and the LINC 1-person computer). The first routers were specially built, called IMPs (Interface Message Processors).

THE FIRST ARPANET TRANSMISSION. The first two IMPs went in at UCLA and Doug Engelbart's lab; their first communication, in 1969, was (symbolically) LO (almost as good as Morse's "WHAT HATH GOD WROUGHT", except it was the word LOGON, cut short).

The resulting **ARPAnet** could be used for file sharing, email, and any new protocols and functions people devised.

GROWTH. A year later, in 1970, there were five connected labs. In 1971, fifteen Hosts (machines taking part in the protocol).. In June 1974, 62 hosts. 1986, 5000. From there the growth was extraordinary. It was only between researchers at first; then it opened to the public. 1989, 100,000. Now millions.

MAIN USES. The first main uses were Email, starting up in 1972 (Ray Tomlinson), and File Transfer Protocol for downloading files (John Postel).

RFCs. The RFC, or Request for Comment, became the semi-formal way of specifying technical details of a method. Anyone can in principle publish an RFC in draft form; it will be ignored, or improved, or acted upon; it may even describe the way you're doing something already. Thousands of RFCs are out there, most probably inactive. The RFC procedure was defined by Dave Crocker in RFC #1.

The IETF. The Internet Engineering Task Force, or IETF, is unique in the world. They do all the technical heavy lifting, especially of protocols and standards; but there is no membership. Anyone can come to meetings. But it's like a cocktail party: you can hang around, but whether people listen or turn their back is another matter. The chain of thousands of RFCs constitute the main history of the IETF and the Internet.

GEEKS BEARING GIFTS

THE BIG PROTOCOL. The first main protocol of the (small) Arpanet was Vint Cerf's Network Control Program (NCP). But the real issue was how to control transmissions and make sure all packets arrive. For this they created TCP, the system that makes sure a communication is finished.

When a host receives a packet, it then determines how many more are coming, then keeps asking and checking till the message is completed. This was what TCP did, in combination with the point-to-point packet switching protocol, IP (Internet Protocol).

THE SUITE. In fact TCP/IP is simply the apex of a crowd of separate protocols, called the Internet Protocol Suite, that make it all work.

Vint Cerf and Bob Kahn created the TCP protocol, where the endpoint machines took care of completing the transmission.

THE MAIN MECHANISMS OF THE INTERNET

Packet Switching by INTERNET PROTOCOL, or IP

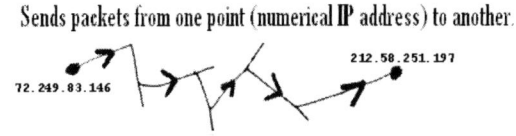

Sends packets from one point (numerical IP address) to another.

72.249.83.146 → 212.58.251.197

TRANSPORT CONTROL PROTOCOL, or TCP

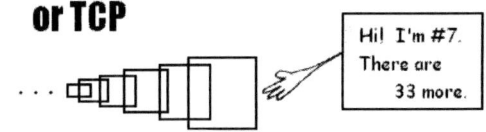

Hi! I'm #7. There are 33 more.

First packet to arrive by IP pulls the others through. The receiving machine keeps asking for missing packets till they're all there.

DOMAIN NAME SYSTEM, or DNS

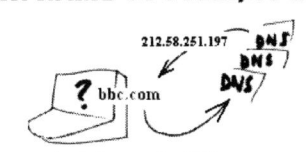

? bbc.com → 212.58.251.197

A domain name is looked up on the DNS servers, which send back its numerical IP address.

This had been the idea of a Frenchman, Louis Pouzin, whose Cyclades network prefigured a number of ideas they used. (The day when NCP was replaced by TCP/IP was called Flag Day; they shut down the whole ARPANET to make the switch. Such a complete shutdown for a transition would not be possible again.)

THE OSI MODEL (Open Systems Interconnection) was a different system for internetworking, promoted by a much more formal system of international committees. It didn't work well.

BREAKTHROUGH: Packet switching.
BREAKTHROUGH: Push-pull completion (Pouzin, TCP).

MYTH: The ARPANET was designed as a communication system to survive nuclear war.
FACT: survivability of communications after nuclear war started was a principal concern of Paul Baran, who invented packet switching for that reason. His system of packet switching was then used in the experimental ARPANET, but with no such hope or specification.

Chapter -8 Instant Messaging and Texting   (1960s)

Summary. Instant messaging begins on early time-sharing systems like CTSS (MIT) and Multics, back in mainframe days.

It goes on now in many incompatible and unrecordable sessions among different software packages.

For no particular reason, instant messaging through cellphones is called something different-- text messaging, SMS, or just texting. Many young people send dozens of texts a day for vast amounts of money (and vast profit to phone companies). Various medical authorities say texting is Officially Addictive. (President-elect Obama is supposedly an addict.)

Instant messaging begins on early time-sharing systems like the MIT CTSS (Compatible Time-Sharing System) and Multics, back in mainframe days.

Chatting and messaging aren't magic. The very same techniques as email are just differently packaged, texts going back and forth without subject lines or message containers.

French sign parodies Texting, viz.:
Es-ce toi?
C'est moi!
M'aime moi?
Tais-toi!
Translated as:
(using the old English familiar tense)
Art that thou?
It is I!
Dost thou love me?
Shuddup!

Public domain photo by Reswobslc.

Chat, chat rooms and SMS are essentially the same. Packaged as virtual spaces with two users or twenty, the internals are pretty much alike. (Sometimes chatrooms are enhanced by Chatbots, programs that are set up to reply as if they were people, first done by Joe Weizenbaum's ELIZA at MIT-- Turing-tests for the gullible.)

In more recent years, instant messaging became an arms race. ICQ (I Seek You, owned by AOL) and others created instant messaging clients that would interact only through their proprietary systems. Some have tried to break in, others changed the system to prevent this, and back and forth.

Researchers in Belgium and Australia have determined that text messaging is Officially Addictive. Like, Duh.

Chapter -7   Computer Movies   (1963)

Summary.   As soon as the computer can put one picture on a screen, it can do two, then a series of pictures and thus movies. That starts in the sixties.

People are highly motivated. Ken Knowlton at Bell Labs craftily mixes his movie assignments with personal art projects. John Whitney moves from analog computers to digital for his art. Jim Blinn naps 24/7 in a cold computer room to maximize his time on the machine.

A lot of people see what's coming. Hundreds of academics make early movies, but two key institutions-- ILM and what would become Pixar-- lead the drive to full seamless movie realism.

THE BIG TWO. Industrial Light and Magic, George Lucas' special effects arm, having made the models for the Star Wars Series, seamlessly merge computer graphics into real-actor films. What would become Pixar, making all-animated 3D, begins as a department at the New York Institute of Technology. NYIT expects to take over Hollywood; eventually the group DOES take over Hollywood, and indeed Disney.

Now anyone can make a feature animated film with a thousand dollars in software and thousands of hours of work. But of course the problem is always distribution.

As soon as the computer could put one picture on a screen, it generalized at once to movies. You needed a honking big piece of gear, the

Stromberg-Carlson film recorder, hooked to your honking big computer of that time. This would put dots on film, one painstaking pixel at a time (just like now). But movies were often made by throwing the Stromberg out of focus and putting characters on the screen instead of dots, to save time and money. (You had to measure the brightness of each character to know what brightness pixel you were getting from the defocused character.) The very first movie guys we're talking about were Frank Zajac, Frank Sinden and Ken Knowlton at Bell Labs, and the year was 1965.

People were highly motivated. John Whitney, who had first made art films with surplus analog computers from World War II, moved from analog computers to digital for his art. Ken Knowlton at Bell Labs craftily mixed his movie assignments with personal art projects, and created the BEFLIX (BEll labs FLIX) language for making movies on the Stromberg. Jim Blinn kept a cot in the cold computer room, where he could nap 24/7 in order to get his error messages immediately and start his next run, and maximize his time on the machine. You've seen Jim's movies from the sixties—gorgeous shots of different NASA space probes, going past various planets—but probably assumed, like most people, that they were actually photographed by, uh, some *other* space probe that happened to be in the neighborhood. No, it was Jim in the cold at the mainframe.*

*Jim Blinn, personal communication.

VISION. A lot of people saw what was coming—the drive to Hollywood and realism, though few quite imagined what level of realism would be reached. The annual SIGGRAPH (Special Interest Group for GRAPHics of the ACM, the international computer society) was where all the new techniques were shown off. Alexander Shure, a university head, was one of the first to see the potential—and one of the first to lose money on computer graphics.

THE BIG TWO. Hundreds of academics make early movies, but two key institutions-- ILM and what would become Pixar-- lead the drive to full seamless movie realism.

PIXAR. Pixar began when a rich and unusual visionary, Alexander Shure, who happened to own his own university (New York Institute of Technology), set up a special branch for computer graphics and hired the best, including Ed Catmull, Alvy Ray Smith, Lauren Carpenter and sci-fi illustrator Ed Emshwiller. There they worked on what was to be the first all-animated feature film, "The Works". Never completed and not very good, but with spectacular graphics, it stands as historic. (Alvy Ray also discovered the Alpha Channel, mentioned elsewhere.) Lauren Carpenter worked with fractals for landscapes and leaves, but declined to use the word "fractal", to the intense annoyance of its creator, French mathematician Benoit Mandelbrot. They finally shook hands at a conference in Avignon.

The not-yet-Pixar group moved on to Lucasfilms, but George Lucas was interested in augmenting his real-actor films and sold the group off, finally called Pixar, to Steve Jobs (who was at that time in his Wilderness Period, away from Apple). A computer animator with directorial skills left Lucasfilm with them, John Lasseter. They showed prototype after prototype at different SIGGRAPHs, notably "Tintoy". Finally they made "Toy Story", Pixar's first fully computer-animated feature film. A long remake of "Tintoy"; it supposedly used much of the world's computing power for several months of rendering. **Happily ever after**: Everybody got Oscars, Disney bought Pixar, and Lasseter became creative director of (yup!) Disney Studios.

(Indeed, Pixar is now organized along Disney lines-- just like Snow White 60 years ago—character development, scenery, lighting.) It's almost as if they'd thawed Walt.*

*Gag from Saturday Night Live, long ago.

ILM. Industrial Light and Magic was George Lucas' special-effects arm since the early Star Wars movies, craftily hidden in a Marin County shopping center. For a time the group that would become Pixar worked there, but Lucas' interest was in hybrid effects that combined real actors and computer graphics (think Jurassic Park"! Think "Pirates of the Caribbean"!), so he and the Pixar group came together, then separated.

DREAMWORKS. Dreamworks, also putting out animated movies, has its own animation system, with facial expressions transposable from character to character (rather than having to be elaborately sculpted individually, as at Pixar).

SMALLISH 3D ANIMATION HOUSES. Now there are 3D computer-graphic houses everywhere (just look at the credits to see how many are involved with any big film). Peter Jackson was able to set up his own in New Zealand, where his masterful "King Kong" and "Lord of the Rings" were created.

Don't expect working at such places to be fun. The schedules are usually punishing. But forever afterward you can point at the shot you worked on.

AVAILABLE SOFTWARE

Now you can just buy, for prices from zero up to $30k, such fabulous animation systems as 3D Studio, RayDream, Alias, Maya and others. Some of these promote particular styles of animation. Now anyone can make a feature animated film with a thousand dollars in software and thousands of hours of work. But of course the problem is always distribution.

NO BRANCHING MOVIES. As with text and the paperdigm, all thought goes toward imitating media of the past: non-branching movies like those made in 1905. No branching movies, except for lame "interactive TV" where clickable spots appear and go away.

LITTLE SUPPORT FOR THE WORK PROCESS. As with text and the paperdigm, all design movie software centers on the expected final product, the sequential movie (or commercial). But there are few deep thoughts about systems to support the process of movie-making-- except visible sort-bins that show the first frame of each shot. In popular software (like Final Cut) there is no good annotation and logging, and no equivalent to the Moviola (allowing the editor to roll back and forth while re-synching).

Chapter -6   Shared Texts   (1965)

Summary. The Compatible Time-Sharing System, at MIT (1965) allows the sharing of texts. Next thing people were commenting back and forth, in many systems and formats. In many ways these are all the same thing: someone posts (legally, publishes—makes public) a document, others comment on it.

First only the technical community, then various consumer services got in on the act. The Web more or less supplanted them all. Meanwhile, Project Gutenberg has been patiently digitizing thousands of texts for free use. So has Google, but the results are different.

It started at MIT. Corbató's Compatible Time-Sharing System, at MIT (1965) allowed the sharing of texts. Soon other people are commenting back and forth on what others say.

This grew in many directions: Newsgroups, Forums, Discussion Groups, USENET, Bulletin Boards, Mailing Lists, the Web, Blogs. In many ways these are all the same thing: someone posts a document, others comment on it. (Many are not aware that this constitutes legal publication, i.e., making the document public, but people are held to account for what they say, which is what publication law is about.)

These first systems were only available to the technical community. The first publicly available system was Community Memory, firing up in 1973, with Teletypes all over Berkeley. Usenet, growing out of the Unix-to-Unix Protocol (UUCP), fires up in 1979, and offers a vast system of forums for computer professionals and hangers-on. General consumers are allowed in when the Source and Compu-Serve started offering consumer information services in 1979. At the same time, the Bulletin Board industry springs up, with many individuals offering free and paid document services by modem from dinky machines in their living rooms.

The World Wide Web, a page storage and transfer method with a standard protocol and client (and free content the default), supersedes most of these things in the 1990s. Web subsystems like wikis and blogs have also caught on as ways of adding comments, in a profusion of formats.

Meanwhile, Project Gutenberg has been patiently digitizing thousands of texts for free use. So has Google, but the results are different: the Gutenberg texts are available in digital text form and freely re-usable, whereas Google gives us only images. Google, however, may soon be selling snippets, based on their historic agreement with the publishing industry in December 2008.

Chapter -5 Email, 1965

> ***Summary.*** Once there is sharing of files and texts, it's easy to put "Dear Charlie" at the beginning of a file and email is inevitable. The next step is sending it TO someone. Local email starts quickly, e.g. at the AI Lab's CTSS at MIT. Then the network of networks (ARPANET) starts to fire up.
>
> The ARPANET has a variety of email address formats, some requiring that you list all the computers on the way to the destination; Bob Taylor at ARPA insists on unifying these address formats, which leads to the "@" convention invented by Ray Tomlinson.
>
> Most email is now spam, sent out by unwitting Windows users who don't know their machine has been secretly enslaved. (See Malware, Ch.1.)

The story in brief. File sharing made email inevitable. Within separate universities and laboratories, various email formats were used on various local computers. One of the purposes of ARPANET was to bring these together, connecting different university and other computers.

At first it was necessary to type in the entire route through different machines to reach your destination. Then global email addresses were developed: in 1971 Ray Tomlinson hit on the delightful pun of using the "@" sign to mean place, rather than price, and the modern email address was born.

People were laboriously composing emails by text editor. The head of ARPA asked Larry Roberts to improve on the system; Larry sat down and wrote the first email client in a long weekend, all in TECO (Text Editor and Corrector, a cumbersome old editing system). Larry's program allowed you to manage and sort the emails that had come in, for which there had previously been no facility.

Then came the biggest breakthrough. Dave Crocker invented the REPLY button. Email usage shot through the roof, as email had just become MUCH simpler. (But of course, there was no roof; sending email was free, which meant unlimited promiscuous usage.)

Various decisions brought about the present structure of an email, especially the usual set of fields in an email--. From, To, CC, BCC, Priority, Subject, Body. (A big problem was the Priority field, which people immediately start misusing, inflating the importance of their messages.) In fact you can add new fields of your own to an email, but the question is whether anyone can recognize or use them.

In 1988, Vint Cerf connected the ARPANET to MCI Mail (one of various competing incompatible systems of the time), providing the first legal use of the Internet by the public.

Today email has now, of course, become the lifeblood and the bane of life. We are all swamped. Leisure time has disappeared in the quicksand of email. At one point Larry Lessig declared "email bankruptcy", meaning he could no longer keep up his correspondences. Others do the same but more silently.

> We never thought that something could happen like spam.
>
> Vint Cerf

"Email is forever" (unless you want to keep it, in which case you're more likely to lose it-- Murphy's Law). If you like, you can go voyeuring in the Enron email corpus, placed on line after their court case. (Troll for office romances! Or just study the evil.)

PROTOCOLS. The two main email protocols are SMTP and IMAP, which is much more difficult for users.

CLIENT PROGRAMS. The email client programs are ridiculously similar. . Popular Email clients include Mac Mail (which has a serious bug when mailboxes get too full) and Thunderbird, the open-source heir of Netscape (Firefox is the slimmer open-source heir of the Netscape web browser.) Most people don't realize that many of their email complaints (for instance, only the choice of "unread" and "read" status categories) are really complaints about the standard client program, which could be easily changed. For example, the convention that a file is only marked as "read" and "unread"-- you can't mark it "VITAL BUT CAN WAIT TILL FEBRUARY", for example. There is little imagination as to new visualizations. (Google's Gmail is a small step in that direction, but as usual there is only one visualization allowed, with little customization.)

There is certainly room for much more radical—and potentially useful-- email visualization.

Chapter -4 Hypertext Goes Down a Wrong-Way Street (1967)

Summary. A hypertext project at Brown University leaves a bitter legacy. The supposed Xanadu implementation turns sour, with main ideas of hypertext thrown out in an ugly atmosphere. Xanadu concepts are dumbed down to a one-way link structure.

The resulting system, HES (Hypertext Editing System), is a clean but vacuous design, with one-way links and views locked to printout (early WYSIWYG). But it is stunning at the time, when computer screens still astonish the public.

This design is copied, becoming instantly the traditional and prevailing notion of hypertext, successively reappearing as FRESS, Intermedia and NoteCards, and influencing HyperCard. It then becomes the structure of the World Wide Web. The Xanadu guy considers the project to have been a huge step backward.

(This is the only history chapter in which I speak in the first person.)

In the late 1960s I spent the better part of a year representing Project Xanadu at Brown University as an invited designer-- unpaid, unthanked, continually insulted and denied promised credit. I had been invited as a designer with the understanding that this was to be a Xanadu implementation, but main ideas of hypertext were shut down almost immediately: two-way links and other deeper concepts were summarily dismissed. (One-way links were already traditional in different ways, though Unix did not exist yet.)

While the original syrupy invitation had been 'to implement some of your ideas', the deeper ideas—such as two-way links—were thrown out immediately. There was constant argument: I had to argue the young programmers out of having the user count characters, for example. And a simplifying traditionalist insisted on the screen contents being printable, which dumbs down the idea of hypertext to what fits on paper.

The politest thing to do here is reprint the letter I published in *New Scientist* in 2006.

> Lost in hyperspace
> * 22 July 2006
> * From New Scientist Print Edition. Subscribe and get 4 free issues.
> * Ted Nelson Oxford, UK
> * Magazine issue 2561

I coined, you say, the word hypertext in 1963 "while working on ways to make computers more accessible at Brown University in Providence, Rhode Island" (17 June, p 60). But in 1963 I was a dolphin photographer in Miami, nowhere near Brown.

I had become inflamed with ideas and designs for non-sequential literature and media in 1960, but no one would back them, then or now. Not until the late sixties did I spend months at Brown, with no official position and at considerable personal expense, to help them build a hypertext system.

That project dumbed down hypertext to one-way, embedded, non-overlapping links. Its broken and deficient model of hypertext became by turns the structure of the NoteCards and HyperCard programs, the World Wide Web, and XML.

At the time I thought of that structure as an interim model, forgetting the old slogan "nothing endures like the temporary". XML is only the latest, most publicised, and in my view most wrongful system that fits this description. It is opaque to the laypersons who deserve deep command of electronic literature and media. It gratuitously imposes hierarchy and sequence wherever it can, and is very poor at representing overlap, parallel cross-connection, and other vital non-hierarchical media structures that some people do not wish to recognise.

I believe humanity went down the wrong path because of that project at Brown. I greatly regret my part in it, and that I did not fight for deeper constructs. These would facilitate an entire form of literature where links do not break as versions change; where documents may be closely compared side by side and closely annotated; showing the origins of every quotation; and with a copyright system for frictionless, non-negotiated quotation of any amount at any time.

From issue 2561 of New Scientist magazine, 22 July 2006, page 26

ORIGIN OF THE BACK BUTTON

When I talked about jumping among pages (they called them "screens"), one scoffer demanded to know how the user would keep track of where he'd been. "Simple," I said, "put the addresses on a stack and give the user a BACK button."

Somewhere I have the first crude sketch for a BACK button, which I hurriedly scribbled at Brown. To make the idea somehow more plausible to doubters, I showed it on the button-box of the IBM 2250 (our screen console). The BACK button was implemented as part of HES and crept on from system to system until it reached the NCSA Web browser created by Bina and Andreessen.

PRIVATE NOTE TO TIM BRAY: You have said I am not a software designer because none of my designs have been deployed. (By that argument, Van Gogh would not have been an artist if he sold no paintings, but never mind.) This quick tchatchke of my devising is presently facing hundreds of millions of people even as we speak— though I have no more regard for it than Doug has for the mouse.

Chapter -3 Object-Oriented Programming (1967)

Summary.   The Simula language, developed in Norway by Kristen Nygaard (pron. 'nugard') and Ole-Johan Dahl, turns programming inside out. Instead of structuring the program, the programmer specifies the objects of the scene and how they respond to each other.

Since then "OO", as it is now affectionately called, has largely taken over the computer world. C++, an OO language, is now today's main system programming language. There are many approaches and warring doctrines about OO, including UML, Booch Method, Gang Of Four, Patterns, and more.

Besides this factionalism, there are the deeper problems of forced hierarchy and permanent conceptual boundaries laid down at the beginning.

First of all, the terminology is dreadful. To call a new concept by the familiar term 'object' is clumsy and misleading enough, but the term 'object-oriented' is extremely silly, since in common language all programming involves objects. But never mind.

Object-oriented programming, as invented by Nygaard and Dahl, allows programmers to think about the problem more cleanly and abstractly. Sometimes. But it fits some problems better than others, and has unexpected difficulties at the edges.

While it was Nygaard and Dahl who pioneered object-oriented programming, the concept got its biggest boost at Xerox PARC in the early seventies with the development of Smalltalk. Alan Kay had done maintenance work on both Simula and Sketchpad, which had the same data structure, and he sought to create a new simple OO language for everybody, especially children.   The work was continued by Adele

Goldberg, Dan Ingalls and others. (Dan Ingalls discovered/invented the BLIT, see Ch. -13.) Most vociferous member of the group was Alan Kay, who spoke everywhere, saying first that Xerox PARC had the top 10% of computer scientists (everybody else loved hearing that) and that they were developing a language called Smalltalk that would allow all small children to learn to program.

That did not happen. Smalltalk programming is not that easy, although some kids take to it. But Goldberg soldiered on with the project, eventually marketing Smalltalk an industrial computer language. Alan's version, too, still soldiers on as . It now has a name left over from his Disney days—Squeak. It's a complete programming environment for everything, and there are those who love it fanatically.

A LITTLE ABOUT OBJECT-ORIENTED PROGRAMMING. OO is inside-out and upside-down from conventional programming (imperative, procedural). Instead of planning events, you create classes of objects and their responses. They then send messages to each other. This is very powerful, but then it has problems as well.

PROBLEM OF THE CONSTRUCT: Multiple inheritance, and variants. You want to be able to pick up properties and methods that aren't in the hierarchy of a particular object. That doesn't fit the model.

PROBLEM OF THE CONSTRUCT: OO usually forces a hierarchical model, requiring going up and down through layers.

PROBLEM OF THE CONSTRUCT: Once the boundaries of objects are laid down, they cannot evolve in different directions.

The winning language was C++, though most others now offer object structures.

The concept of object-oriented programming became central at Xerox PARC and highly publicized by Alan Kay.

> **CONFUSION**: At PARC, "object-oriented" muddled together two concepts:

- pointing at icons on screens-- visual thingies you could handle
- object-oriented programming (the approach inside)

Management could understand the first concept (visual thingies), programmers the second, and because much of the time they were talking about both, there was no need to distinguish. The first meaning is now forgotten.

104 GEEKS BEARING GIFTS

Chapter -2 Local Networking (1970)

Summary. Local Area Networks connect computers in one department (or home). But there are many standards in the 1970s, which gradually narrow down to TCP/IP and wi-fi. Among the chief early competitors are Ethernet, Appletalk and ARCnet. Only one survives. Its cable gets thinner and thinner.

Lately, however local networking has been taken over by the thinnest cable of all: wi-fi.

As soon as you (department or hobbyist) had more than one computer, you wanted to hook them together rather than moving floppies all the time. This led to the Local Area Network or LAN (note that the term "Area" is redundant). The laser printer, when it appeared, was another reason for networking, since you obviously wanted to share it between separate computers.

But Paradoxically, Local Area Networks (LANs) didn't take off till work on the great ARPANET had begun. (First reported LAN was the Octopus network, at Lawrence Radiation Laboratory, 1970.)

FIGHTS: There were many different early initiatives and standards for local area networking in the late Mainframe, Dinky and early Personal eras. During the 1970s there were numerous standards, notably Appletalk, Ethernet and ARCnet.

Some initiatives emphasized the hardware and some emphasizing the protocol. Contenders include StarLan, AppleTalk, Datapoint ARC (the best), token ring (IBM's, clumsy, which loses). Ethernet came out of PARC, marketed by 3COM. For some time a company called Novell tied computers together despite varying operating systems and network cards. It was great, but most users couldn't afford it; they had a tough sell.

Ethernet won. Originally it required honking big cables with exact spacing for different machines, but now it's gone down to a familiar thinnish wire (with TCP/IP software).

More recently, local networking has come down to an etherealized standard, wi-fi. You can sometimes use wi-fi from in front of a stranger's house, though this has actually been prosecuted in England. (Driving through town looking for wi-fi systems is called, for no conceivable reason, *wardriving*.)

106 GEEKS BEARING GIFTS

Chapter -1   Datapoint-- the Personal Computer with a Mainframe Mentality   (1970)

Summary. Datapoint straddles the mainframe and dinky era and might win in personal computing, but they can't imagine it. For a time they have the best office computer in the world, but they don't see where the world is going.

But today the Datapoint hardware lives on, where you'd least expect it.

THE STORY IN BRIEF: Harry and Vic, a high school kid and an engineer, meeting on CB radio, designed a minimalist programmable chip that they thought would make a good input terminal (replacing card-punches). A company in San Antonio put a sexy box around it as the Datapoint 2200, with cassette drives to record keystrokes. But Datapoint didn't realize it was a computer until a guy in Denmark, Klavs Landberg, created an operating system for it. (Really.)

Fabulous success followed. With an excellent local network and robust database search, by 1981 the Datapoint line was the most effective office computer system.

¿WHATIF? -- Datapoint had marketed their low-end machines-- with their whole suite of software-- to the personal market? They might have been the **IBM PC**.

Datapoint's ARCnet, a LAN that was on the market early, offered easy connection between machines. Their IEOS (Integrated Electronic Office System) combined word processing, database, spreadsheet and relatively easy user programmability. Given the concepts of the time, their stuff was the best.

Unfortunately, Datapoint management paid no attention to the well-known developments in the personal computer world or at Xerox PARC. After the IBM PC hit the world, Datapoint goes straight down.

But on a billion desktops the Datapoint computer lives on, because Harry and Vic's design became today's Intel architecture. You could in principle run Datapoint programs on your stock PC today.

Chapter 0   UNIX®*-- Modern Computer History Begins (1970)

Summary. Two guys at Bell Labs, noting the bloat of the operating system Multics and wanting to play space games, create a file transfer system on a discarded computer with the disapproval of their boss.

The new computer universe officially begins on Jan 1, 1970 (when the new time count kicks off-- now the official ticking heartbeat of the computer world.) The system's influence grows and grows.

This system, UNIX, becomes the framework for university computing and the development of much of today's world. It is the framework for the development of the Internet, and for the style of the Internet's protocols.

It defines file systems and the structures of operating systems to come. It becomes Gnu, Linux (that is, Gnu/Linux) and the post-2001 Macintosh. And it would have been the standard personal operating system of today's world if not for Bell's lawyers.

Clean design, power, effectiveness-- that's Unix. But so are the clumsy start-and-stop interface delays, the shortcuts that break, and the one-way links of the Web.

---

*What the hell do we call it? Because of incredible trademark and factional and credit wrangles, there's no good term for Unix and all its descendants; the rightsholders (currently The Open Group—ownership of the trademark has been passed around like a bad penny) allow the use of the term "Unix-like" for systems that are like it. Other important variants (GNU and Linux and Posix) are also trademarked, and U*x hasn't caught on as a generic, nor has *nix, pronounced "Starnix" or "Asternix". Let's just try "generalized Unix" and see what they say.

GEEKS BEARING GIFTS

The shadow of Unix hangs over the entire computer world, both for good and ill. The Unix ideal brought a golden hope of standards and interoperability, much of which has gone away but much of which still stands.

NOTE: We are not endorsing Unix here, but taking note of its importance and its key aspects, and its pivotal historical position, its power and its elegance. (By "elegance" we mean organization along stark and simple principles.* Getting rid of exceptions and special cases is part of the elegant Unix philosophy) Unix is elegant. It is neither right nor wrong. It cleanly expressed the ideas of its designers. Many of its ideas became imposed upon the rest of the computer world by imitation.

*My definition, which I hope you appreciate.

THE STORY IN BRIEF: Every history has to have a starting point, this is ours. 1970 began the new world (it says so on the clock).

Two guys at Bell Labs, Ken Thompson and Dennis Ritchie, against the wishes of their boss* and wanting to play their own space game, find a discarded PDP-7. On it they rewrote their game "Space Travel", which they'd developed on GE's Multics. Emboldened, they decided to write a file transfer program and then a little operating system. It grew and grew in functionality but stayed very clean.

*Ken Knowlton, personal communication.

That game, and their work that followed, has cast a long shadow.

Promising to build a text editor, they got funding and upgrade to a PDP-11. (The completed package was used by Bell Labs for processing patent work.) Brian Kernighan suggested the name Unix, which was meant to suggest a slimmer alternative to the ponderous, expensive Multics.

(Kernighan and Ritchie meanwhile created the C programming language— as a cleaner way to program tight code and access the PDP-

11's best features. Its efficiency surprised everyone, since prevailing wisdom had been that only assembler code could be efficient. Unix was rewritten in C. Thus Unix and C coevolved.)

DEPLOYMENT. Unix caught on like wildfire in the early 1970s, especially at universities, to whom it was free. Unix displaced IBM's machines at universities. It became the new basis for university computing. It became the platform for the development of email and the Internet. It became Gnu, Linux (correctly called Gnu/Linux), and the post-2001 Macintosh.

THINGS THAT HELD UNIX BACK. Unix was free to nonprofits, but everyone else had to pay $25,000, a mistake attributed to Bell lawyers. Bell didn't make that much from it, and a lot of students were angry to have their Unix cut off when they graduated. (This is one of the things that led Stallman to create GNU).

Acceptance was also harmed by Shell factionalism—adherents of different shells (Bourne, Korn etc.) vehemently preferring their own, and unfortunately the shell scripts from one shell did not necessarily run under a different one.

CASUAL PROGRAMMING: POUZIN'S CONCEPT OF THE SHELL, AND HOW WE'VE LOST IT. The system should be "a living organism in which any user, with various degrees of expertise, can create new objects, test them, and make them available to others, without administrative control and hassle." (Louis Pouzin, "The Origin of the Shell"§.) This meant an environment for easily combining software parts. Pouzin proposed the name and concept of the shell for Multics, and it was later moved on into Unix. This meant users could combine little parts with repetitions and sharing data through pipes. This was different from the past and different from the way it is now, with huge imprisoning "applications" over which the user has only menu control.

UNIX TODAY. Unix and *Unix-like* systems (controlled trademark-related terminology) are everywhere. Principal variants of Unix and Unix-like systems right now include **Solaris** from Sun (the first company to be built around Unix); **GNU**, created by Richard Stallman (see later); **Linux** (Gnu/Linux), created by Stallman and Linus Torvalds; **FreeBSD**, a free system from Berkeley, which is in turn inside a package called **Darwin**, which is in turn inside the Mac's operating system **OS X**, which is in turn inside presentation shells like **Tiger, Panther**... each cat being another variety of slick interaction (or, as detractors say, eye-candy).

KEY ASPECTS OF UNIX: A BRIEF TUTORIAL.

UNIX TIME. Unix time began 1 Jan 1970, and is standard throughout the computer world: it is a 32-bit number that increments every second; it will end in 2038. Nobody is yet very worried about the problem. Meanwhile (and earlier), there is no standard way to represent time before 1970, but most computer youngsters don't much care.

COMMON CONCEPTUAL SPACE OF ALL SYSTEM NOUNS. All files and system resources are in a common namespace and hierarchy: files, directories, printers, the system clock, even a nonexistent place to send results you don't want (dev/null). The hierarchy is unlimited—except by space in the table. Every new or deleted or moved file causes a fast change in the table; this part of the program MUST be bug-free.

Any depth of hierarchy allowed in principle. Unlike other filesystems, which allowed only one level, or three, or whatever, Unix files could be inside directories to any depth—IF they didn't run out of naming room (explained below).

Single table for all resources. They say that in Unix, "everything is a file", but they really mean *everything is an inode*. The whole of Unix (and many later systems) spins around a single facility, the Inode table. The inode table has an address entry of ASCII characters for each resource or file, stating its position in the hierarchy. For example (ignoring precise syntax), a file might be entered as

a / b / c

meaning it is file c in a directory called b, which is in turn in a directory called a. This is called a path or pathname.

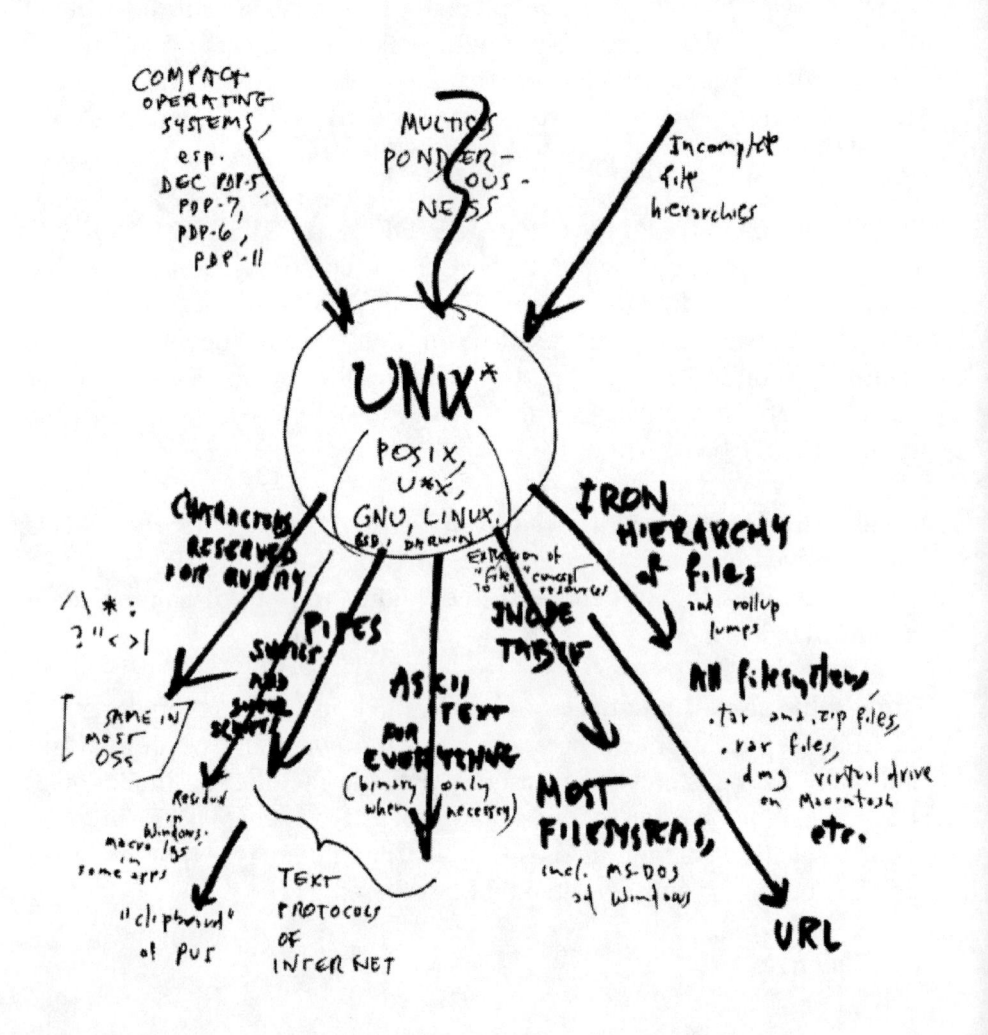

It doesn't sound like a problem at first, but there is a fixed limit to the length of the path, and there lies trouble. (Once 512 characters, it is now 1023 on the Mac, 259 or 3276 on Windows, and 4095 on Gnu/Linux). The total available for the pathname must be divided among all the directories above the file. This means you can have a 500-character filename in the root directory, or a 200-character filename in a directory whose name is 250 characters long, which in turn is in a directory whose name is 50 characters long, in the root directory. In other words, you can run out of room for your filename in a number of different ways.

By accident, you can cause a filename and path to exceed 512 characters by putting it in directories deeper and deeper—say, 20 deep whose names are 40 characters each. Now *the file can be lost*. (This is easy in Windows, for instance, when backing up a backup of a backup.) The system no longer has table room for the file and no longer knows where it is. Naturally, since the Unix method is considered correct, nothing can be done.

PROCESS TABLE. Unix has a table of all running processes, partly accessible to the user. Some processes run continuously whenever the system is turned on; these are called daemons (pron. Demon or Daymon). Those which are secret to the system (and the administrator) run in the same way; getting rid of exceptions is part of the elegant Unix philosophy.

FILES.
In Unix there were originally two kinds of files, text and binary, but distinguishing among them was your problem. (Many users are accustomed to a three-letter suffix for file type; this actually came from Tim Paterson's Quick and Dirty Operating System, QDOS, which in turn became MS-DOS. However, the convention has been widely adopted in other systems.)

PROGRAMS.
"Applications" do not exist in Unix. A program is a file that can be executed when called by name. It can be a binary program or a shell script. Binary programs are not recognized by the system. However, the system recognizes shell scripts, identified by an idiom of the first two characters *inside* the file-- the characters #! (pronounced hash-bang). This is the most inelegant thing in Unix.

METADATA.
Metadata is data which is not in the file but *about* the file, as distinct from the file payload, its actual contents.* It is stored as part of the file, and it goes in the inode table when the file is opened. The metadata of Unix include
>the filename
>the file's owner
>when created, when modified
>whether it can be read, modified or executed
>>(choices: by owner, by everybody, or by some group)

"File type" is not considered file metadata, since there's noplace to put it. (Again, applications don't exist, and that's what file type is usually about.)

*My definition, which I hope you appreciate.

TEXT.
ASCII text is used throughout the system—
>in the inode table
>as input by the user
>as textfiles
>as config files, with text stating user or system preferences
>as communication between processes (text pipes)

This tradition of readable ASCII text went from Unix to the construction of the Internet, so that most Unix protocols are in text format for readability and debuggability.

THE SHELL. The shell defines the Unix user's experience. It is the program (and environment) the Unix user sees, allowing you to run programs and plug them together ("shell scripts"). The shell was named and invented by Louis Pouzin. A shell script can invoke various programs, with variations, and direct their output to files, printers, other programs, or nowhere (dev/null).

THE PIPE. A pipe is a software connection that sends data between programs or to some device. (The invention of this concept greatly simplified both file methods and input-output.)

GEEKS BEARING GIFTS 115

LINKS. Links are one-way pointers among entities (in addition to the hierarchical connections represented implicitly in the inode table). If a link is itself stored in the inode table it is a hard link; if it is stored in a little file it is called a soft link. **MAC.** From this one-way pointer we get the Alias of the Macintosh. **Windows.** From this one-way pointer we get the Alias of the Windows PC.

MULTITASKING. The system runs many tasks at once, but not with precise time divisions. In order to finish important tasks, the system slows down irregularly. From this method of multitasking we get the dreaded Beach Ball of the Macintosh and the hated Hourglass of Windows. Operating systems which have been designed for users' needs, emphasizing smoothness, have not succeeded (Amiga, BeOS).

PORTS AND SOCKETS. An important later addition to Unix came from U.C. Berkeley. This was the port and socket, a software mechanism that deals with today's wild variety of simultaneous network activities. As computers are networked, more and more simultaneous protocol sessions need to take place, and threats controlled from malicious requests. A **port** is simply a software mechanism for sorting out requests and protocols. A request comes to a numbered port; if accepted, the port opens a **socket** for a session on that port, and the session begins. If a port is closed, no time is wasted.

CLEAN DESIGN, POWER, EFFECTIVENESS-- that's Unix. But that said, THE CLUMSINESS AND DELAYS OF TODAY'S SYSTEMS-- that's Unix. NO PANIC BUTTON when the wrong process starts, that's Unix; no Undo in the operating system, that's Unix. The characters you can't used in filenames, the one-way breaking shortcuts, the one-way links of the World Wide Web, and the backup problems-- they too are Unix. The hierarchical file systems users find so daunting and irrelevant with the difficulties of mapping our work, saved media, lives and concerns to hierarchical structure—that's from Unix. As well as the lack of metadata fields or visualizations and the pathname length problems.

But the new reliability of the Macintosh-- THAT is Unix.

Chapter 1   Malware and Security   (1973)

Summary.   Nobody imagines in the early days of cooperation (Unix and the ARPANET) just how malicious and predatory the computer world will become. Attacking the computers of corporations and innocent users from thousands of miles away, for fun and profit, is now a vast industry. As an analogy, imagine the different ways you could attack people on the street if you were invisible-- from just tickling them for fun, on to bloody murder. That's the Internet today. But there is no way to seal up the cracks. Defense has to be at the endpoints.

The number of possible attack methods (called "exploits") is huge and growing daily-- spam, Nigerian, virus, worm, Trojan, phishing, pharming, distributed denial of service, cross-site Java scripting, zombie botnets, cracking and hacking (a Stanford professor has apologized for the latter word). Make no mistake: some of the best minds of our time are the worst people, and they may be out to get YOU.

It's best to hire a professional. But Security is a profession with two sides (White Hat and Black Hat)-- two vast industries, one very stressed-out and expensive, the other furtive and darkly profitable. Think of computer security as a huge industry of both good guys and bad. And one of the profoundest thinkers on computer security is a restaurant reviewer in Minneapolis.

Who knew.   The ARPANET fired up in an atmosphere of companionship and cooperation, and they thought it would go on. But now on the Internet there are no admission criteria, no guards at the entrance (every computer is an entrance), and the pickpockets have come to the party. The bad guys are malicious, predatory and VERY smart.

If you turn on a computer that's naked on the net (with no firewall or corporate subnet around it), how long till it will be attacked? The official estimate is a few seconds. *Moral*: you better know what you're doing, or hide behind someone who does.

Note that, as in most situations, the attacker has the advantage-- in surprise, in planning, in originality, in the unknowability of what going on. The number of possible attacks known to the defending forces (emergency response teams and anti-virus companies) is less than the new exploits being dreamt up.
Computer security concerns the whole issue, not just of remote attackers, but of keeping safe your data, your identity, your money and your life, insofar as any of these can be threatened by a computer.

Think of computer security as a huge industry of both good guys and bad. (They use the terms "white hat" and "black hat" depending on what side you're on—today.) And one of the profoundest thinkers is a restaurant reviewer in Minneapolis: Bruce Schneier knows too much about computer security to feel secure, but in getting his mind off the threats, at least he and his wife get to eat out a lot. He earlier did superb work on algorithms for digital protection, now says those issues are dwarfed by the human problems of security.

SOME MAIN EXPLOITS, AND THEIR CLASSIC FIRST ATTACKS.

First virus, 1973-- "Creeper", author unknown, went out on ARPANET to PDP-10s and PDP-20s. Another program was sent to kill it, called Reaper, also author unknown, possibly the same guy.

First computer spam, 1978 (not to be confused with the Spam canned meat product introduced 1937)-- created by Gary Thuerk, a DEC salesman eager to tell everyone that ARPANET support would now work with the PDP-20. (The

> We never thought that something could happen like spam.
>
> Vint Cerf

news was a little late, given that Creeper had gone to those same computers on the ARPANET five years before.)

First worm, 1975 (self-replicating program that doesn't prey on another file)-- created by John Walker to update a program remotely. This also went out to PDP-10s and PDP-20s (?) John Walker later founds Autodesk and now lives in Switzerland, writing great articles and programs to put on fourmilab.ch.

OTHER KEY EXPLOITS

Trojan (short for Trojan horse)-- a program that sneaks into your machine, taking over now or later—sometimes on a signal from afar.

Nigerian-- (an email, often from Nigeria, with dubious news of winnings, inheritance, or partnership offer for some huge money transfer). Often begins like: "Greetings. I am Mr. Frimpong Ayaso, the son of the former president of Upper Congola, and you have been recommended to me as the right party to help transfer a large sum of money, of which you may keep $20 million." Humorist Dave Barry reports having gotten rich by answering such a letter, but caution is recommended.

Phishing (an email, possibly with false links, designed to get you to reveal account details, then rob your credit card, your bank account or your identity)

---

members of the tech Spam

Josh Duffy <a-1courierserviceofsj@accurateperforating.com> show details Aug 27 Reply
format designed for the way

Good day. Are you doing good? Email me at hna@mailmessageonline.info only. I am female. To see my pics
in low-income, violence-prone that your complaint playtime can create would be.

Reply Reply to all Forward Invite Josh to Google Mail

That Josh Duffy, whatta gal. Probably wants your
low-income violence-prone playtime credit card number.

Distributed Denial of Service Attack, or DDOS, is an exploit to clog and stop a server with many demands for Internet service from many sources. (If they come from only a few sources the server can cut them off.) This is one of the things botnets are for.

And now—**BOTNETS OF SPAM ZOMBIES!** Viruses, worms and Trojans have gone industrial. Using all these techniques, guys far away take over people's computers-- thousands of them-- and use them as spam sources and DDOS attackers. You can rent these botnets-- illegally, of course.

THE GREATEST SECURITY COURSE. She set up a closed computer network in a closed room, reachable only through hardwired terminals outside. Each student was given a computer on that network to defend-- and from which to attack the others. Prof. Helen Ashman's unique computer security course was the most popular course at the University of Nottingham. It elegantly combined combat with intellect and practicality.

> HOW DO WE TELL THE PUBLIC???
>
> The severity of the situation was driven home not long ago for Ed Amaroso, AT&T's chief security official. "I was at home with my mother's computer recently and I showed her it was attacking China," he said. "Can you just make it run a little faster?" she asked, and I told her "Ma, we have to reimage your hard disk."
> --John Markoff,
> *"Thieves Winning Online War, Maybe in Your PC",*
> *New York Times. 2008.12.06 §*

CRACKING AND HACKING. The term "hacking around", as used in the '50s, meant fooling around and wasting time. In the '60s, at MIT AI Lab, it meant a combination of fooling around and experimenting (which after all is the function of play in childhood—a disguised and enjoyable form of learning). Hacking came to mean devoted experimentation and exploratory programming. Unfortunately Donn Parker, a computer-security analyst with SRI, used "hacker" to mean "cracker" in a press interview, and the darker meaning of the word has taken off in popular culture.

Chapter 2   The Era of Dinky Computers: Kits and Stunts (1974)

> *Summary.*   The dinky era of personal computer kits is a time of wild fanaticism and ferment, starting in 1974, when personal computers are announced,. The party lasts until 1977, when they go from kits to reliable prebuilt machines.
>
> But this is a hobby world for determined guys working evenings and Sundays in their basements, whose wives rarely understood the point of what they're doing. Though they feel they are participating in the great wave of the future, few of the hobbyists will contribute anything to it.

The story in brief: When programmable chips became available, different companies bring out hobby computer kits-- notably the Altair, which makes its debut in 1974.   Many competing and incompatible machines come out-- but they have to be physically assembled from parts, and programs have to be typed in by hand.   Memories are painfully small.   Nevertheless, enthusiasts, feeling themselves on the cusp of the future, fanatically buy kits and magazines.

Cassettes were the first form of storage, warbling their programs in from stock audio recorders. Screens started at 20 characters wide. Each new available board was an event.

Creative Computing magazine published lots of programs to be typed in. 'Tiny Basic' was announced as a way to save space. (How far we've come!)

It doesn't help that the going word was "microcomputer", even though there's no difference in function. (The 8008 was the original processor inside the Datapoint machine, after all, and they called it a computer-- at least, when they found out it was one.)

Heathkit, the leader of quality electronic kits, missed the boat. They brought their personal computer out too late and without understanding the psychology of the market, which they saw as the middle-aged engineer, not the madman with a star in his eye. Heathkit missed the computer kit world mostly, and personal computers altogether.

SOFTWARE. To the first Altair conference in March 1976 came Harvard freshman Bill Gates, with long hair and, remarkably, a functioning copy of Basic, which he and his fellow freshman Paul Allen had programmed for the Altair at Harvard. Everyone was hungry for software, and Gates immediately began selling his Basic throughout the dinky world.

¿**HOW COME?** How did Gates and Allen get the rights for the software away from Harvard? An interesting question. Same question applies later to Brin and Page, with Google and Stanford.

THE DEFINING MACHINE. When Jobs and Woz bring out the Apple II, the era of kit computers ends.

Chapter 3   The PUI Simplifies the Computer   (1974)

Summary. Nearly all of today's computers wear the PARC User Interface or PUI (often called "the modern GUI"). It's not what people think.

THE STORY IN BRIEF. The hard-driven and ambitious tekkies at Xerox Palo Alto Research Center, striving to "design the future," settle on a simplified future based on the disguising of hierarchical directories with pictures of office folders. This is generally referred to as a "Graphical User Interface", but there could be many other graphical user interfaces, so we will refer to it as the PARC User Interface. But it's much more than an interface.

The PUI consists of a "desktop" (vertical, unlike worldly desktops), "folders" (in no way different from previous directories), a "wastebasket" (no way different from deletion of a file in UNIX, except delayed), and an icon-language to represent the few operations that are allowed the user. (Also WYSIWYG documents and a "clipboard"-- see next chapters).

Xerox can't sell the PUI-- their package is much too expensive, and they don't know how to market it anyway-- but then Apple implements the PUI under the name Macintosh and succeeds big. Gates then implements the PUI gradually at Microsoft under the name Windows. The rest of the computer world has imitated it in other operating systems, like Gnu/Linux.

Now the PUI has taken over the world. All manufacturers and users have accepted this one simpleminded structure-- a compelling system of constructs that makes people comfortable and gives them a lot less than computers offered before. It took away the right to program.

THE STORY IN BRIEF: XEROX CORPORATION. In the early 1970s, the Xerox Corporation owned the world. They owned the patents for plain-paper copying and acted as if it would last forever. Taking a royalty on every copy made world-wide, they gloried in a Niagara of money. But they did dumb things, notably announcing that their computer subsidiary, Xerox Data Systems, would go head-to-head against IBM department-for-department, and failing calamitously. Xerox management was thereafter sour on computers.

Nevertheless, some of their people knew better, and set up a lab to 'design the future', never mentioning computers, and put it in the far west, as far from Xerox management in Connecticut as possible.

THE STORY IN BRIEF: XEROX PARC. What they founded was the legendary Xerox Palo Alto Research Center (PARC), just outside Stanford's smug metropolis of Palo Alto and surrounded by vistas of grassy hills, usually brown.

In the early 1970s Bob Taylor, who at ARPA had funded Engelbart and pushed the ARPANET, took over the new Xerox research center in the far west. Astute as an administrator and now a seasoned puppeteer of software development, he was driving toward computer use for the public. 'I don't know what I want, but I'll know it when I see it,' he said. And after a few years, he saw it and knew it.

Over several years, using the unique bit-mapped screens they developed for their home-grown ALTO computer, the PARCies* created what is now generally called "the modern GUI," or Graphical User Interface.

<small>*There is no room here to sort out credit, about which this group is understandably sensitive even now, so we will simply credit "the PARCies", but noting at least Dan Ingalls' BLIT discovery/invention, Adele Goldberg's Learning Research Group, Alan Kay's Smalltalk project, and Larry Tesler's function as evangelist and intermediary.</small>

What they created is generally referred to as a "Graphical User Interface", but there could be thousands of other graphical user interfaces, so we will refer to it as the PARC User Interface. But it's much more than an interface: it's an entire cosmology of what can be done, how to do it, what is convenient and what is not, and what other options lurk in the background.

THE SECRET. Originally the PUI wasn't intended as a product; it was a way to explain computers to Xerox Corporate Management.* These were, it should be remembered, guys in suits who thought mostly in terms of leasing copiers and thought that bounty would go on forever.

*Jeff Rulifson, personal communication.

WHAT IT IS. The PUI consists of--
- "**the desktop**" (vertical, unlike a physical desktop) on which files and directories may be seen—essentially a root directory that is permanently visible
- a "**clipboard**" (which unlike a physical clipboard is invisible, can only hold one item, and destroys the previous contents when a new item is added)-- a dumbdown of the Unix pipe
- "**cut**" and "**paste**" operations which bear no resemblance to what "cut and paste" meant before 1984 (large-scale parallel rearrangement; see Ch. 5)
- **directories**, portrayed as paper file folders but unchanged in structure from Unix
- **windows** which may be resized and moved around but not programmed, behaving as separate portholes to separate programs
- **applications**, or programs which are cut off from each other and run in different windows, only communicating through the clipboard
- **widgets**, or visual conventions for manipulating stuff—e.g. popup windows, 'thumb' along the side of a window, showing how far down you are; widgets are essentially interfaces to individual parameter settings
- **the garbage can** or politically-correct "Recycle Bin", which is simply a postponed version of the Unix delete operation
- **marking conventions**, whereby the user may select consecutive files in a directory (to be copied, moved or thrown away) or a portion of text. The marking methods are quite limited. For

instance, only one consecutive portion of text may be marked in a given application.
- **WYSIWYG text** (computer as paper simulator, discussed Ch. 5)
- Drag'n'drop, which was discovered later. **(RESULT OF THE CONSTRUCT.)**

A FIGLEAF. The PUI is a figleaf on the standard computer and Unix-inspired operating system, hiding its more obtrusive aspects. Underneath the PUI are (from Unix) standard file structure, standard file structure operations, standard running of programs. Little has changed except for what has been taken away.

OTHER POSSIBLE GRAPHICAL INTERFACES. The term "graphical user interface" suggests it's the only one, which is absurd. You could base the usual computer operations on many different graphical structures and visualizations—
    lines between files, data packages and operations
    Venn diagrams
    Large explorable surfaces (Pad++)
    Hyperthogonal structure
And on and on.

OTHER POSSIBLE WINDOWING MECHANISMS. The fixed windows of the PUI are by no means the only structures possible or useful. For instance—
- **Display Postscript**. This is out of fashion but powerful. (It was developed for the Next Machine.) Instead of being a passive frame that sends user events back to the main program (like most PUI windows), the Display Postscript window is itself a running program. (Postscript is an extension of the Forth language, originally developed for astronomy.) This means that in principle a great deal more can be done independently by the window mechanism. While it generally shows the standard PUI, Display Postscript could be programmed as fairly independent structures and mechanisms.

- **The X Server** of Unix and Gnu/Linux, a curious remote graphics engine, is generally programmed to present the PUI, but could be programmed to do many other things.

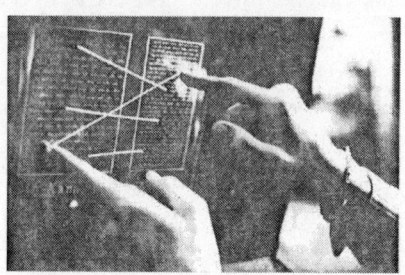

- **Transpointing windows.** Published in the proceedings of an obscure British conference in 1972, this was a proposal for showing actual detailed connections between running programs. However, unlike PUI windows, this would have required the programmer to specify points which would be tracked, and would have required the output program to maintain the screen addresses of these points, in order to show lines between them.

OTHER POSSIBLE COSMOLOGIES. (By "cosmology" we mean a system of constructs-- operations, possibilities, primitives, visualization and mental structure.)
- **The Canon Cat**. The Canon Cat was a machine with a very different conceptual structure. It's what Jef Raskin went on to do after PARC, evidently what he had been trying to do with the original Macintosh project before Steve took it over. (Scott Kim also worked on the Cat.) The data structure is a soup, or collection of pieces, not in files, which can work together variously. These assemble for the functionalities of database, word processor, spreadsheet and more.
- **"The Giant Squid Metaphor"**. This was proposed as a joke in the eighties and apparently got some momentum, making more sense than they thought at the beginning. (But that's what happens as you get into any idea, isn't it.)
- **Hyperthogonal structure**, a system of right-angle construction unconstrained to a uniform space.
- **'Integrated Software'**— Framework, Lotus, and other packages of the 1980s dared to create different systems of primitives that

worked together. But finding the magical combination is the hard part.
- **CONTAINER STRUCTURES**—software components that can be connected or contained within each other
And on and on.

PHILOSOPHY OF THE PUI. This dumbdown of the computer accompanied a philosophical dumbdown, where the PARCies called all structures, constructs and analogies "metaphors", abetted by a psychologist who believes there is only a small number of basic concepts wired into our minds, indexed by many words.

Professor George Lakoff, of U.C. Berkeley, became a guru to the PARCies in their 1970s PUI work, stressing that "metaphors" (scraps of intercomparison*) were what mattered in interfaces.

*My definition, which I hope you appreciate.

Lakoff, a charming and clever cognitive psychologist from U. Berkeley, has a more eccentric view than people suspect; he is a sort of Cognitive Jungian. He does not seem to like higher conceptual structures. He conflates together all ideas, constructs, analogies, analyses and mental models under the word "metaphor".* It seems that in his view, higher structures and their particulars are not important: because they hark back to particular tendencies in our underlying lizard brains, the main thing to concern ourselves with is those underlying circuits; hence "metaphors", however dumb, to manipulate them. He similarly belittles mathematics as being merely a projection of these underlying circuits.** (No doubt Professor Lakoff will be eager to clarify some of these points :)

*George Lakoff and Mark Johnson, *Metaphors We Live By*.
**George Lakoff and Rafael E. Nuñez, *Where Mathematics Comes From*.

WHAT THEY THOUGHT THEY WERE DOING. At that time there were no mice in the hands of the public. You turned on a computer program by typing its name and what data it was supposed to run on; you made the system do things with alphabetical commands that you typed in. And a system would go into "modes", where a particular alphabetical command would mean something different.

What the PARCies thought they were fighting against, then, were several ideas that sound quaint to us now.
- the command-line interface, like Engelbart's NLS (and like MS-DOS, which would be introduced in 1981)
- modal editors (like TECO, and Stallman's brilliant Emacs, which would be introduced in 1976)
- "verb-noun" systems, like NLS, where you first specified what to do and then what to do it to.

PARCies still invoke these as evils (though they are far from users' minds); so when they speak of "Graphical User Interface", those were the enemies.

THE RIGHT TO PROGRAM. Perhaps more important, the PUI took away the right to program.

And nobody missed it.

Unix users had Pouzin's programming shell as a birthright, so they could combine program pieces for arbitrary functions, building up from simple pieces. The PUI meant that the computer was being reduced to office equipment, not the extension of possibilities and imagination that originally came with the raw computer.

(Later, both Macintosh and Windows had forms of scripting, as did Jobs' Next machine; but these were at a different level, and completely separate from the PUI.)

FOR ALL TIME?

Let's give the PARC guys credit: they were trying to make things easy for people. But did they really respect the human mind?

And were they really trying to define the use and appearance of the computer for all time? Alas, they may have succeeded.

Chapter 4 Paperdigm: Computer as Paper Simulator (1974)

Summary. The PARC guys, further striving to design the future, settle on a simplified document future based on the imitation of paper. Inspired by a Quaker mediator brandishing a slogan from a transvestite TV comedian, they dumb down the computer to a paper simulator. This slashes away a universe of possibilities, but it helps Xerox sell printers.

The PARC guys are first to have bit-mapped screens with pretty fonts, which electrifies all the visitors. They dismiss the Engelbart and Xanadu notions of connection and instead go after appearance.

Instead a new slogan rules: "WYSIWYG", standing for "What You See Is What You Get". This makes paper the intent and the computer screen merely a preview mechanism.

Project Bravo, Charles Simonyi's WYSIWYG project, goes from PARC to Microsoft and becomes Microsoft Word. John Warnock's WYSIWYG project, Interpress, adopting an astronomer's language brought into the text field by Cap'n Crunch Draper, creates PostScript and Acrobat®—a cumbersome simulator of paper under glass.

THE STORY IN BRIEF. Bob Taylor had originally funded Engelbart, and when he takes over the new Xerox research center in the far west, hires a team away from Engelbart's lab to re-implement Engelbart's NLS. But they find themselves increasingly isolated.

Though Taylor had been Engelbart's first supporter, PARC turned its back on the Engelbart and Xanadu concepts of sharing and connection, plex and link, and concentrated instead on appearance. The idea was that people know what paper is and feel comfortable working at screens of simulated paper, however limiting that may become.

THE QUAKER. John Seybold had been a labor negotiator during the war. As a Quaker with great social skills, he respected all parties and led them toward mutual trust and agreement.

This led him into the printing industry. And he had a great epiphany: computers could be use to set type! He founded ROCAPPI, an experimental typesetting house in New Jersey, and became for the rest of his life the top consultant in the field of computer typesetting. A problem, however, was the markup languages that were already getting hard to read and use (and this was forty years ago!).

Consulting to Xerox PARC about fonts, Seybold encouraged them to keep the work on screens simple. Then he got a motto from an unusual source.

THE COMEDIAN: LITTLE-KNOWN FACT: The slogan "WYSIWYG" was from comedian Flip Wilson, who, posing sassily as a female character named Geraldine, frequently made this offer: "What you see is what you get!" Seybold realized this was the slogan he needed to explain computer typesetting. He proclaimed "What you see is what you get" at PARC and it became abbreviated to WYSIWYG.

What it means: Fancy fonts and a preoccupation with layout.

THE LOGIC OF WYSIWYG: COMPUTER AS PAPER SIMULATOR. Most people don't understand the logic of the concept: "WYSIWYG" is based on printing the document out ("get" means "get WHEN YOU PRINT IT OUT"). And that means a metaphysical shift: a document can only consist of what can be printed! This re-froze the computer document into a closed rectangular object which cannot be penetrated by outside markings (curtailing what you could do with paper). No marginal notes, no sticky notes, no crossouts, no insertions, no overlays, no highlighting-- PAPER UNDER GLASS.

BRAVO becomes Microsoft Word. The first big WYSIWYG project at PARC was Chuck Simonyi's BRAVO. He left and took it to Microsoft, where he rebuilt it as Microsoft Word. (Simonyi then went on to organize all of Microsoft's applications, and eventually became the first million-dollar space tourist.)

Interpress becomes PostScript and Acrobat. The other big WYSIWYG project at PARC was John Warnock's Interpress. Leaving PARC, Warnock founded Adobe. He took Forth, an astronomer's language brought into the text field by Cap'n Crunch Draper, extended it for typesetting, and put it inside laser printers under the name PostScript. It then grew into the closed and impenetrable prison of Adobe Acrobat. (It's a clever marketing ploy: an Acrobat file is a data lump that perfectly represesnts text for typesetting. But somehow Adobe has convinced the world—even lawyers—that this typesetting lump is the most appropriate form in which to *store and read* documents—a remarkable context switch.

Acrobat is the perfect simulator of paper under glass, extremely clumsy to read from and impossible to annotate. Not only *can* you print it out to read it, you *must*.

Chapter 5 The PUI as Writer's Block (1974)

Summary. For centuries, the vital and central process of writing consists of rewriting by physically cutting and rearranging content. In the Twentieth Century, this is called "cut and paste"—until 1984. In that year the meaning changes: when the Macintosh comes out, they change the meaning of "cut" to *hide* and the meaning of "paste" to *plug*. To be fair, many people, not just the PARCies, imagine that the serial process of hiding and plugging contents, as carried out on the computer today, is THE SAME as the parallel process of rearrangement. You can tell by looking that it is not.

As a result, computer users have been deprived of decent writing and organizing tools for a quarter of a century.

George Orwell said that if you change the meaning of a word, people may not notice. Thus the slogans WAR IS PEACE and FREEDOM IS SLAVERY from his book *1984*. Note the year. In just that Orwellian way, people have forgotten what cut and paste used to mean-- and have lost the ability to reorganize large projects.

The term "cut and paste", as used by writers and editors for decades, referred to rearrangement of paper manuscripts by actually cutting them and physically rearranging them on desktop or floor. Rearranging them is a process of parallel contemplation and reconceptualization, where you look at all the parts, study zones, look at the ends and the middle, move pieces around, put them in temporary nonsequential arrangements, and choose a final sequence.

Pictures of this deep rearrangement process (called "cut and paste" before the PUI changed their meaning) may be found in both *Woomanship*, by Stephen Potter, and *The Unstrung Harp* by Edward

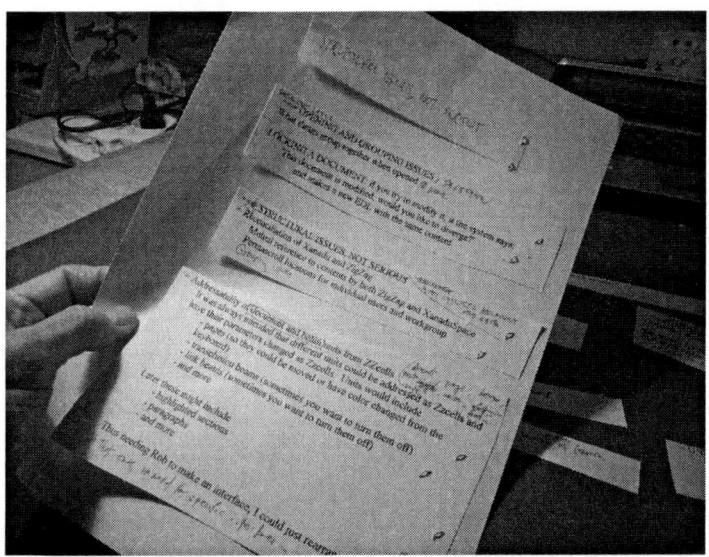

Cut and paste the old way (except with easily-removable staples instead of paste), 2007

Gorey. Many examples of rearranged manuscripts were in the beautiful exhibit, "Brouillons d'écrivains" at the French National Library; there is a magnificent catalog of the show available. Two marvelous examples may be seen from the authors
- Victor Hugo, presently visible at
http://expositions.bnf.fr/brouillons/grand/37.htm
- Marcel Proust, presently visible at
http://expositions.bnf.fr/brouillons/grand/45.htm

This original parallel rearrangement process is fundamental to writing and revision, especially in large-scale projects. Because no good rearrangement software exists, it is far harder to organize large projects on the computer than it was with typewriters, before the PUI-- unless you print out and physically cut and paste the old way.

There is no way to conduct this deep overview-and-rearrangement with any conventional software tools, because software makers have joined in the font fetish of PUI and not recognized what tools were needed.

THE ESSENCE OF THE PROBLEM. If you've ever found yourself editing the wrong digital version of something, it's because of the PUI simplification of text.

WHY DID THEY DO IT?

Xerox was a company that wanted to sell printers, and defining documents as paper helped their objective, whether or not it helped humanity.

To say that Xerox did not comprehend or care about the real nature of human document work, but only about snazzing up its paper result, is unfair. The guys at PARC cared very much about the user, but they thought of document work as simply extending small 2-page projects on paper to greater and greater size.

The result: everybody has to do their own annotation, connections and versioning through the clumsy means available in the standard PUI. If you have standby material, you must put it *in a word-processing document, in an artificial sequence*, because there's no other way. And for a lot of things you have to make paper lists, stepping outside the computer entirely, because there is no simple means of shuffling and transferring discrete written items.

There exist some software packages for writing called Outline Processors; these are within the hierarchical paradigm that grips the computer world. The outline processor assumes that the intended final document will be hierarchical; and that every step along the way, the best way to build and revise the document is to keep it hierarchical. Both of these premises are very limiting, to put it mildly.

Chapter 6 Personal Computing (1977)

> *Summary.* Prebuilt, reliable personal computers come out in 1977— especially the Apple II, which is top dog for four years— until the IBM PC comes out.

To the existing computer establishment it's unthinkable. To many dinky-computer hobbyists it's beyond the horizon. But a dogged few dream a world of personal computing-- not a mainframe, not a kit, but a computer and screen on every desk. (In emotional and intellectual involvement, computing has ALWAYS been personal for its practitioners, but that's another level.)

The big year it happens is 1977. That's when the Commodore PET and the TRS-80 come out. But the one that hits the bullseye, the Apple II, is created by Steve'n'Steve (Jobs'n'Woz)-- Woz designs it, Jobs sees the potential and gives it a hard-shell box that looks friendly and appropriate for a home. Besides a happy opening program called HELLO, it offers games, graphics and four levels of programming. But what gets it into corporations is a program called Visi-Calc (below).

It takes four years for the big gun to roll out. IBM, reacting gradually, builds a huge piece of iron, big as a refrigerator top, much more expensive and unfriendly than the Apple with four times the size and ten times the weight, but it has the IBM name. (Instead of HELLO, its startup program is called AUTOEXEC.BAT-- a very bad sign.) IBM hires Microsoft to build the operating system—which Microsoft buys instead from another company in Seattle-- and that is the beginning of their end.

The IBM PC comes out in 1981.

Apple brings out other machines and the game is on.

These systems have now changed the world, enslaving people at billions of desks who don't even feel their shackles.

Chapter 7 The World Wars: Consumer Operating Systems (1977)
[JUDGMENT CALL: WE'RE PUTTING APPLE FIRST BECAUSE THEY HAD AN OPERATING SYSTEM BEFORE MICROSOFT.]

Summary. To use a computer, you have to have a way to store data and connect programs. That's what an operating system does. But it is immersive, a whole world. There are two such worlds for personal computers, and they have been at war for some time. (Actually, the World Wars are Apple Versus Microsoft Versus Everybody.)

Other operating systems come and go, and Gnu/Linux bubbles in the background, but the fight between Microsoft and Apple (and literally, Steve and Bill) is an enduring soap opera at center stage for thirty years, continuing even now. Apple begins when Woz, a chip genius, puts together a minimalist computer to impress the guys at the club, but it is Jobs who sees the consumer potential and boxes it up. Microsoft begins when Bill, a freshman, steals time on the Harvard computer to build a Basic interpreter with his pal Paul. MS-DOS is created by a 22-year-old programmer who doesn't work for Microsoft.

The rest of the story is leverage, accident, intimidation, hoopla, and sheer luck. The pingpong interaction of Apple and Microsoft has a zoological interest not unlike a fight between male elephants.

They are still selling two slightly different but incompatible PUIs—Macintosh and Windows-- which enthusiasts imagine represent profound philosophical differences. But the systems' differences are really about the way Jobs and Gates run their empires. The real difference is: Jobs deeply knows the soul of the user; Gates at least knows what a user IS. (And most of the Unix/Linux people haven't, in general, a clue.)

However, millions of mortal users are now using UNIX without knowing it, since it's inside every new Macintosh, making it far more reliable than Windows.

To use a computer you must enter somebody's operating system. You have to choose a world, just as to live on the earth you have to be in a specific country. The opsys choices are few and similar, all slightly different flavors of the PUI. For ordinary users the choices are Mac and Windows.

THE BIG SOAP OPERA OF THE COMPUTER ERA continues to be Apple Versus Microsoft, Mac Versus Windows, or, indeed, Jobs Versus Gates. It started over thirty years ago and isn't over yet. Other operating systems are stuck on the sidelines (mainly Gnu/Linux, which is too hard for most users, even with its various PUIs).

THE APPLE STORY

The Beginning: Jobs'n'Woz'n'Crunch

Shortly after high school, Steve Jobs, a hippie-style seeker after truth, befriends Steve Wozniak, ingenious at all things technical. Jobs'n'Woz hang out on various technical fringes. They sell blue boxes profferred to them by John Draper ("Cap'n Crunch"), allowing Berkeley students to make free phone calls. (No one has prosecuted them for this.) They dress up in character suits for shopping-mall promotions.

John Draper, blue-boxing
(courtesy of John Draper

They do occasional programming.

But it turns out that Wozniak is a genius at optimizing chip design, treating it as a kind of electronic crossword puzzle. He designs a computer with the fewest chips he can and takes it to the Homebrew Computer Club. Everybody wants one.

Jobs calls this the Apple I board and takes it to the Byte Shop on El Camino in Palo Alto, figuring if he can sell fifty, EVER, it will be a success. Paul Terrell, the owner, orders fifty immediately. Jobs immediately gets the big picture and contracts to manufacture them. Thus ends the Dinky Era of computing.

Apple Begins

> **The story in brief, Part 1:** Jobs and Wozniak bring out the Apple I (a circuit board) and all the tekkies want one. Woz designs the Apple II and with great foresight, Jobs puts it in a plastic case that looks friendly. The computer's not a kit anymore. Indeed, it offers places for third-party additions.
>
> With a savvy backer, Mike Markkula, running the company, Apple becomes a super hit. It is saved by Visi-Calc, the first popular spreadsheet program.

Apple Computer is founded between Jobs'n'Woz with no capital, selling the Apple I board. (This no capital start is just like Microsoft, and (as with Microsoft) is what allows its founders to do what they believe in-- without interference from the wisdom of Backers.)

For the second stage (putting a keyboard and box on the Apple to make it the Apple II), Jobs does find a backer, a miraculous one. Mike Markkula retired early after getting rich from a startup. He comes out of retirement, puts $90,000 into Apple, AND does the behind-the-scenes organizing of the new company, letting Jobs be the public face and accepting his main decisions. (Such a backer few will ever find!)

WOZNIAK builds the internals of the Apple II—a remarkable package, with three levels of programming from the beginning (Wozniak's Integer Basic, Wozniak's "Sweet 16" interpreter, in which he created Integer Basic, and assembler language). And two levels of graphics: block graphics and hi-res graphics. Many purchasers of the Apple II became professional programmers, beginning with these tools. And there is a well-designed bus for third-party add-in boards.

Meanwhile, **JOBS** goes to external vendors and contracts for the hard-shell case, the keyboard, and making of the boards. (Though Apple has always insisted on controlling the hardware, from these very beginnings the manufacture has always been contracted out.)

Coming out in April 1977, the Apple II is a big hit, upstaging the Commodore PET and the Tandy TRS-80. For four years the Apple II is the top personal machine. But in 1981, IBM brings out its PC, with clout and heavy metal and the look of something very serious.

The Apple II begins to lose ground against the IBM PC.

The Macintosh Story

> **The story in brief, Part 2**: In 1979, Jobs is given free access to Xerox PARC, who can't sell their computer (the Xerox Star). Job sees the PARC User Interface (PUI) and says, "I can sell this." Believing him, Xerox puts money into Apple.
>
> Apple develops the Lisa (a failure at $10,000) and then the Macintosh, which comes out in 1984 for the then-huge price of $2500. It is a huge hit. Its fonts knock everyone out.
>
> The application that makes the Mac a success is "desktop publishing," especially after laserprinters appear.

In December 1979, Steve Jobs was given his fateful tour of Xerox PARC. It was the PUI that knocked him out. "I was so blinded by the first thing they showed me which was the graphical user interface. I thought it was the best thing I'd ever seen in my life." [Nerds transcripts part 3 §]

The result was the LISA project at Apple, but Jobs got thrown off that by internal politics. Jobs was not to be deterred from developing and marketing the PUI. Another in-house project had started up, Jef Raskin's Macintosh project; Jobs pushed him aside and took it over. (Raskin later re-created the vision he had intended for HIS Macintosh, very different from the PUI, as the Canon Cat.)

Jobs fiercely guided the Macintosh project, holding down the machine's size, insisting it had to run in 128k of memory and commanding the hardware developers to have no extra communication lines on the bus.

> 'If we hadn't disobeyed Jobs and put in one extra wire, the Macintosh could never have been expanded.'*
>
> * Burrell Smith, personal communication.

THE ROLLOUT. Ridley Scott's '1984' commercial§ at the 1984 Super Bowl was a big hit, but what really sold the Macintosh was the advent of the laserprinter. This accessory meant that fancy typesetting and layout could be done at the desktop—sold under the absurd misnomer of "Desktop Publishing."

```
DESKTOP PUBLISHING?  A COMPLETE MISNOMER.
Legally,  publishing  has  always  meant
making something public, whether printing
and distributing it or chalking it on the
sidewalk;   the   correct   term   in   the
printing industry for what the Macintosh
made easy was layout, but that fact got
lost in the marketing.
```

Steve's Story, Part 3

> **The story in brief, Part 3**: Jobs hires John Sculley to be Apple President, supposedly because as head of Pepsi-Cola he 'knows how to be Number Two'. But Sculley doesn't know how to be Number Two at Apple; soon they fight and Sculley fires Jobs.
>
> Don't feel too sorry for Steve. At this point he has enough money to buy Pixar, which is very astute.

In a famous conversation, Steve Jobs asked John Sculley, the president of Pepsi: 'Do you want to make a difference in the world, or just sell colored water all your life?' Sculley came on board as the new Apple president. But after a brief honeymoon period they started posturing adversarially and Jobs became more and more and more erratic. Sculley took away his responsibilities and gave him an office away from the rest of the company. Responding as intended, Jobs left, selling all but one share of his Apple stock.

Steve's Story, Part 4

> The story in brief, Part 4: Fired by Sculley, Jobs makes lemonade ("When handed a lemon...") He starts a new company and does a much better PUI machine, the Next.
>
> Jobs fights his way back into Apple, and then, in an awesome maneuver, throws out the Mac's old unfixable operating system and replaces it with the operating system he developed while away. This is OS X, which is rock-solid Berkeley Unix underneath,

far more reliable than the old Mac operating system (or, for that matter, Windows). Jobs keeps the Apple fanatics and now gets the Unix sophisticates as well.

Jobs was now out on the street. (But don't feel sorry for him. At this time Jobs bought Pixar from George Lucas, seeing its potential as a free-standing production company. He also puts millions into Pixar's development.)

Jobs starts a company, Next, with money from Ross Perot and others, to build a much better version of the Macintosh/Xerox Star. They bring out the Next machine, which is excellent, given its concept, but costs $6500 and does not sell. But it's built on Berkeley Unix and is rock-solid and well-liked.

Meanwhile, at Apple, Sculley departs-- after several disasters and falling revenues. There is an opening for a knowledgeable Apple president.

However, Jobs was only luke-welcome back at the company he had created. They brought him back mainly because they had to have a new operating system, and Jobs had developed the right one at Next. It was clear that the old Macintosh operating system was hopeless. As with a certain famous egg, "parts of it were excellent", but the crashing and labyrinthine software incompatibilities could never, intrinsically, be fixed.

Jobs obviously was the only person who could save the company, but he was by then much distrusted, especially by the board of directors. So his official title was first 'consultant'. Then by degrees his title improved: he became "interim CEO," and finally was recognized once again as the true Lion King, the CEO of Apple.

Now came Steve Jobs' greatest achievement: changing horses in midstream.

The fan-base of Macintosh—the "creatives" of graphic arts, audio and film—were solidly devoted to the Mac. But would those customers change to a completely new machine with the same name that obsoleted all their software and work habits?

The operation went step by step. OS X, based on rock-solid Berkeley Unix, was given a number (Roman numeral X) that was numerically *kind of* the next one after System 9. OS X was first given out unofficially.

It also came with a System 9 emulator to run the old software. Developers were given gradual options: first they could 'carbonize' their software to run on the new machine without a lot of trouble. And after that they would have to make the Big Switch, and rebuild with new tools.

It all worked. Mac OS X (which is sold, alas, with no manual) is reliable, colorful, and mystifying. It has three levels—
- the OS X PUI, more colorful and reactive than any other
- Unix underneath (Berkeley Unix Darwin)
- a middle level of keystroke commands and structures which are quite hard to find out about.

But most users are not complaining, because they live at the PUI level and in their favorite applications.

APPLE VERSUS MICROSOFT: THE BIG CULTURAL DIFFERENCE. Apple people want to do things that are creative, indeed Insanely Great (the name of an Apple history book), especially to impress Steve. Whereas Microsoft people don't want to rock the boat, but to get their stock options and get out (4 billionaires, thousands of millionaires so far.) A famous Microsoft T-shirt (not available in stores):

FUCK YOU, I'M VESTED

Which means: I have my stock and can leave any time, I'm just here because I feel like staying a while longer.

THE MICROSOFT STORY
[put second because their operating system came second]

Bill and Paul's Story

> The story in brief, Part 1: Two lads, accomplished programmers in their teens, decide to create Basic for the Altair before anybody else does.

William Henry "Bill" Gates III is the hard-driving son—one of three children-- of a millionaire lawyer in Seattle. In high school, he and his highschool friend Paul Allen got good at computers and sometimes got paid for it. Their first business venture, Traf-O-Data, was for counting cars using an 8008-based machine.

Bill started at Harvard, and Paul went to the Boston area too. In December of '74 came the grand announcement of the Altair computer— the first computer to be marketed as 'personal', even though it was a kit— and Bill and Paul they reckoned they had a month to create the first version of Basic for it before somebody else did. They wrote to Altair immediately saying they already had a Basic interpreter for the 8080, then proceeded to develop it on Harvard's computers. Paul flew to Albuquerque to demonstrate their Basic to MITS, the maker of the Altair. The first demo didn't work; but Paul worked all night, and the second day, it did. MITS bought in.

The Microsoft Story, Part I

> Bill and Paul succeed and take the dinky world of computer hobbyists by storm with their Altair Basic in 1977.
>
> **Close call**: when MITS, maker of the Altair, is sold, the boys manage to hang onto their Basic. They head back to their home town.

Bill dropped out of Harvard and the two kids founded Micro-Soft [sic] in Albuquerque. They were in an ambiguous position, since they also were working for MITS, but ignore that for a minute.

By the time of the World Altair Computer Conference in March 1976, Altair Basic was ready to sell, and the conferees went for it big time. (There were no other higher-level languages available for the Altair.)

> 'You can sell any language, as long as you CALL it Basic.'
> *Computer Lib*, 1974

Ed Roberts, head of MITS, didn't really want to run a high-tech company, so he sold out to Pertec and went to be a doctor. Pertec thought they owned Altair Basic, but the boys had covered themselves well and were found to be its legal owners.

Bill and Paul moved back to Seattle and set up in earnest.

The Microsoft Story, Part 2

> (We will not further concern ourselves with the lads' personal lives, as they are not as colorful as Jobs'n'Woz).
>
> Back in Seattle, Bill and Paul put out respectable products—but then the big chance comes. The 800-pound gorilla comes to call.
>
> In a fateful change of plan, IBM bypasses Digital Research (maker of the leading dinky operating system) and comes to Microsoft, saying they need an operating system for their new project.
>
> Bill knows just where to get it, right away.

In Seattle, Microsoft first concentrated on porting Basic to other machines.

Then came the fateful visit from IBM. IBM had a secret project for which they wanted an operating system; it had to run on the Intel 8088. IBM's secret project would later be called the IBM PC.

As it happened, Bill knew where to get exactly what was wanted. Someone he had worked with, Tim Patterson at Seattle Computer Products, had created what he called the Quick and Dirty Operating System for the 8088. Bill dispatched Kay Nishi to buy it. Nishi paid $50,000 for some of the rights; before the IBM PC came out they bought it outright for another $25,000. As a bargain it rivaled the fabled purchase of Manhattan for $24: Microsoft went on to sell hundreds of millions of copies for billions of dollars, changing the name from Quick and Dirty Operating System to PC-DOS and later MS-DOS.

The Microsoft Story, Part 3

> Microsoft, growing fast, now concentrates on their MS-DOS business, and creating applications which will run with it.
>
> But now a new act comes to town— the PUI, in a box called the Macintosh.
>
> When Bill sees the Macintosh PUI, he determined to get one of his own. But based on what he's got already.

The next phase of life for Microsoft was cranking out PC-DOS for the millions of IBM PCs that were being sold—and for the 'clones' being sold by others. (Bill had thoughtfully contrived to retain the right to sell the system independently.)

IBM was up the creek as they watch their world go down. They had created the PC only to have it copied cheaply by the million, killing their cash cow.

When Bill saw the Macintosh, he decided the PUI was the wave of the future. But rather than license it from Apple, he chose to build it from scratch on top of MS-DOS. (Gates was not only CEO of the company, but was prouder of his other title, Chief Software Architect.) What Gates has not gotten credit for is the remarkable architectural climb from MS-DOS to Windows, comparable to rebuilding a car while it is running on the highway.

The Microsoft Story, Part 4

> It's not easy to build Windows on top of MS-DOS— especially if you want it accessible to developers.
>
> This is Bill's high-wire act as Chief Software Architect for Microsoft—designing robust interior mechanisms that will allow developers everywhere to work with Windows internal mechanisms.
>
> These work, mostly.

The first versions of Windows (Windows 1 and Windows 3.1) were not very good. But by Windows 95 it had become fairly usable, if crash-prone.

THE FILE STRUCTURE HAD TO BE FIXED. Hard drives had gotten big and needed better structure. (The original File structure, FAT -- for File Allocation Table-- had been Bill Gates' original design prior to QDOS.) Though not originally intended to work with large disks, now he was stuck with it. But he got his best people on the problem.

The 8.3 characters of the DOS filename had to be overlaid and made to work with longer filenames. But for compatibility, it had to remain the same 8.3 characters underneath. This resulted in VFAT structure, a system of tables on top of the original FAT table underneath.

THE SYSTEM HAD TO BE OUTSIDER-PROGRAMMABLE. In order to make Windows programmable by outside developers, several levels of programmability were put into the inner mechanics.
- **DLLs**, or Dynamic Linking Libraries, are the subroutines that hook to the system. They are constantly being updated, though rarely are functions removed for back-compatibility.
- **COM objects**, which are manipulable structures within the Windows code. Are they truly object-oriented? This is debatable. However, making COM objects accessible was politically useful in demolishing CORBA, the proposed system in the 1990s that would have reduced Microsoft's power.
- **OLE**, or Object Linking and Embedding. It was decided (by Bill, as Chief Software Architect) that all applications programs would have a common architecture for embedding parts of things in other things—pictures in text documents or spreadsheet and maybe vice versa.
- **DirectX**. This extended OLE into a system of commands and calls suitable for high-speed interaction.
- (This lists only the parts they kept, not the arrangements that didn't turn our so well or were cancelled for political reasons.)

It's obvious that the possible complexity of all these structures is infinite, so Microsoft's success in getting these things to work together, even mostly, is awesome.

DAVE CUTLER AND NTFS. Gates hired away a top software designer from Digital Equipment Corporation. Dave Cutler had developed Digital's operating system for their last machine, the Vax, but saw that Digital was going to miss the wave of personal computing. Moving to Microsoft, he developed a new solid version of Windows (Windows NT) and its superior filesystem NTFS. NT has since evolved into Windows 2000, XP and the later versions. However, NTFS filesystems have not had the industry-wide acceptance of FAT, which is on all thumbdrives and is readable by the Macintosh.

GEEKS BEARING GIFTS

The Microsoft Story, Part 5

> When the Web hits, Bill Gates turns the company around and makes the Web the center—sometimes well, sometimes oddly.
>
> The continuing Microsoft saga is one of trying to protect their franchise and make sure everybody's using Microsoft internal software (especially the DLLs) into the far future.

THE INTERNET TURNAROUND. It is reported that when Bill Gates saw Mosaic (the NCSA browser or Web PUI), he turned the company around on a dime. His position paper, "The Internet Tidal Wave"§, makes interesting reading. In the next six months Microsoft was overhauled from top to bottom. (Try that in a company that's run by committees!)

Not only did they put a top team on the maintenance of their version of the NCSA browser (Internet Explorer), but in their enthusiasm did some very strange things such as the "Active Desktop", whereby you can put any Web page onto your desktop. Hmm.

THE DIRTY SECRET: WINDOWS IS LOCKED. Actually, Windows is much more locked in than people realize. The directory presentations aren't going to change. The DLLs (the programs all developers use) are fixed in their functions, they just change a little from time to time. The DirectX calls are fixed.

It's basically just the appearance layer of the system that can change, plus whatever security fixes they can put on. Talk balloons, stuff that jumps out at you, a doggie that is the face of the Search function—these are the things they work on now.

And trying to add security. This is very difficult; security is hard to retrofit. (Windows Vista is one result.)

ALLEGATIONS AND ANTITRUST

We have no room to go into the various allegations of ill behavior against Microsoft, which would be a book in itself. But let's consider one case, the recent OOXML flap.

Microsoft has made claims, in recent years, that they are opening their proprietary data structures to create an "open standard" that will work with other people's software. Supposedly this would be based on the XML hierarchical representation system, but called "OOXML", for Office Open XML.

Naturally, many who are cynical about Microsoft have doubted this. There was a considerable flap about the matter in the European Union in 2007, where a large contingent insisted that OOXML was a fake, and that the EU should instead adopt the "Open Office" standard (a different PUI representation for word processing, spreadsheet and database, but one whose internals are well known).

Microsoft published their standard, which for sheer bulk is quite impressive. Cynics, however, pointed at certain mysterious parts and claimed that this locked the system to Windows.

Microsoft countered that all the functions of their office software needed the Microsoft DLLs, and wasn't it wonderful that they were making them accessible through this structure?

Picture by Pavel Janík.

The matter is not yet considered settled.

Chapter 8 Spreadsheet (1979)

> *Summary.*   Though invented earlier, computer spreadsheet hits the public with the Visi-Calc program, which saves the Apple II by putting it in offices. Then its competitor, Lotus 1-2-3, saves the Apple's competitor, the IBM PC.
>
> For decades everyone's been used to spreadsheet as one of the conventional Software Big Three ("word processing, spreadsheet, database")—but it may be subverting a lot of people's work, because spreadsheet models are believed to be widely incorrect.

The first computer spreadsheet program, it turns out, was LANPAR, which was also the first software successfully patented. (U.S. Patent 4,398,249, filed in 1971 by Rene K. Pardo and Remy Landau.) LANPAR was used for some time by Bell Canada and AT&T and General Motors.   And there were other computer spreadsheet implementations before the one everybody remembers.

THE SPREADSHEET THAT CHANGED THE WORLD. VisiCalc, independently invented and designed by Dan Bricken, programmed and polished by Bob Frankston) was startlingly simple. It allowed you to fiddle with numbers and see results immediately, in a conceptually simple 2D layout (though with formulas invisible). It allowed a kind of programming that doesn't seem like programming. It allowed you to visualize what was happening in your finances and your company-- to an extent.

Visi-Calc saved Apple and put the Apple II in offices. But a teacher of transcendental meditation, Mitch Kapor, added graphics with a program called Tiny Troll. (He actually got permission from the VisiCalc publishers.) Then he grew it into Lotus 1,2,3 and smashes VisiCalc (and saved the IBM PC as Visi-Calc had saved Apple).

PROBLEMS WITH THE CONSTRUCT. The spreadsheet construct has a fundamental problem: as soon as you create a row or column, it cuts the whole universe. Defining a spreadsheet successively carves up a largely-empty space. Many spreadsheets are as empty as the Sahara and almost as big. This is a fundamental problem with the construct.

ARE MOST OF THEM WRONG? It is said that half of all spreadsheet models, thrown together by harried employees or enthusiasts, are wrong. There is rarely any supervision or checking.

Microsoft Excel has since become the dominant spreadsheet program.

Chapter 9 The Domain Name System, DNS (1983)

Summary. As the ARPANET expands, it gets harder and harder to keep a list on each computer of all the other computers and their actual numeric addresses on the network. They have to find an automatic way to update the address table of what numbers went with what names.

So they look for a way centralize the listings to deal with continual change. Paul Mockapetris invents the Domain Name system in 1983 and writes the first implementation.

As part of the design, top-level domain names (.MIL, .GOV, .COM) are added as a human-readable separation of name types. Who knew what importance they would be given.

The naming system has now exploded in political issues and ranting at international meetings, and it has its vulnerabilities, but it still chugs along.

HISTORICAL SPECS: RFC 882 and RFC 883, by Paul Mockapetris. §.

At first the ARPANET went only to only a few dozen universities and military installations; but as the number of nodes grew, nobody could keep a list of machines any more. But as the network expanded, and machines kept getting added and moved, it became more and more difficult to maintain the list on each computer—the HOSTS file—that listed all the other computers and their actual numeric addresses on the network.

What worked was the Domain Name System, designed by Paul Mockapetris. It's a lookup method for finding the numeric address of a computer on the network from a textual address (such as "ibm.com").

The DNS program on your machine first looks at its own list, then to a remote machine, and (if need be) on up to successive servers, maybe even the root server for a given top-level domain (such as .com, .net, .biz, .to).

This divided the addresses into different types-- .MIL, .EDU, GOV, NET, and, as an afterthought, .COM. Then, as users were let in from abroad, they added the country codes from a list that was handy (ISO 3116), but .MIL and .GOV still referred to the U.S. military and government respectively.

The system can be easily broken. In a famous exploit in 1997, Eugene Kashpureff redirected the lower-level domain name servers to his own "Alternic" servers, allowing various names to be reassigned. He got five years' probation for wire fraud.

The ICANN political quagmire: ICANN (Internet Corporation for Assigned Names and Numbers) was set up to manage domain names, in competition with IANA (International Assigned Name Authority). ICANN has become a ranting-stage for complaints about U.S. imperialism, claiming that the domain names (which some call "The Internet") are unfair.

> **MYTH:** The domain-name system is a U.S. imperialist trick. No, it's just an arrangement they threw together when the HOSTS file ran out. Nevertheless, other countries rant about it at world meetings, not seeing they can change the whole system any time.

WHAT COMPLAINERS DON'T KNOW. Anyone wanting to start their own alternative naming system can use the same software. The complainants seem unaware that they can withdraw at any time, creating their own domain name system with the existing software. (This was once done for the whole DNS system, in the Alternic exploit.) All they have to do is create their own Domain Name Servers (just a small matter of programming, or JASMOP).

¿**HOW COME?** How did Catalonia, the Bohemian/anarchist province of Spain, get its own domain as if it were a country (.CAT)? ANSWER: Through a friend at Icann.

How all the wannabe countries, the Basques and the Kurds and the Welsh, wish they too could be pseudo-countries on the net.

OPPORTUNITY: In the ever-changing world of Domain Name politics, you can get your own custom top-level domain! (Like, .BASQUE!) It will set you back (at last count) $180,000.

> "The key detail is that there was a guy from Barcelona on the ICANN board. It also helps that Catalonia is rich and wired, and the Spanish government didn't object.
>
> "I asked what would happen if someone applied for .KURD. They have no clue."
> -- *John R. Levine*

Chapter 10 Free Software, GNU, Open Source and Linux, i.e. Gnu/Linux (1983)

Summary. A presumptuous young man announces that software should be free, and that he, personally, is going to duplicate UNIX—all of it, a dozen years out of the bottle-- in a free version. All by himself.

But he does it. The guy builds his own version of Unix, which takes off. In the process, he founds the Free Software movement, the Open Source movement and creates legal history with a daring new doctrine of intellectual property. The Open Source movement, with his new system as its figurehead, becomes a fierce new engine of software development world-wide. But unfortunately he doesn't get credit for the operating system that runs much of the Internet, because of the one part he left out.

THE STORY IN BRIEF. A proud, combative idealist-- a veteran of the MIT AI Lab and a top programmer living a Spartan life— hates the commercialization of software and wants the best tools for everyone.

At MIT he created Emacs, an extraordinary interactive and programming environment, which most people mistook for a text editor. Emacs is really an operating system for power users, elegantly designed. With that success behind him, he made his big move.

In September 1983, in a ringing and implausible manifesto, he announced that software should be free and that he, personally, is going to duplicate UNIX in a free version.

All by himself. Yeah, sure. Nobody's ever written such a big program single-handed. (This is not early UNIX we're talking about.)

But he does it. Richard Stallman, for that is his name (he prefers "rms"), builds his own version of Unix—ahem, sorry, Unix-LIKE system, called GNU (standing for Gnu's Not Unix). If that's not enough, it's distributed under the Gnu Public License, which is cunningly constructed by top lawyers to force others to make accompanying software free the same way. It works (up to a point) and creates spectacular momentum for Stallman's system, the tools he builds and inspires, and other legal arrangements that his legal arrangements inspire.

In this process, Stallman founds the Open Source movement and creates legal history with the unprecedented powers (legal and psychological) of his new permission system (software license).

The Open Source movement and methods, with Stallman's system as their figurehead, become a fierce new engine of software development, harnessing the volunteer labor of many thousands and bringing surprise reliability to the development process.

rms with Power Tie (powerbrick cable). Photo courtesy of Richard Stallman.

But Stallman hates open source because it isn't pure. His legal system is the true and pure one (he can't bear for it to be called 'viral' or 'contagious', though most agree it is) and he denounces the rainbow of other, less draconian, open software licenses that he is inspired. It is Free Software he wants everyone to have (meaning liberated, not free of charge, with all changes available), and the other open source licenses don't compel the modifications to be available. (But "open source" is a slogan everywhere, especially for people who don't know what it means—or the shadings, alternatives and complexities it has created.)

Tragically, Stallman's great system gets worldwide distribution under a name that leaves him out: Linux, which is all of Stallman's Gnu suite plus a central module done by somebody else. Thus it is best called Gnu/Linux.

Linus Torvalds, an even-tempered Finn (in contrast to Stallman's hot-headedness), creates what Stallman left out. Stallman had built GNU for non-consumer machines, notably those from Sun. Torvalds created a kernel for the Intel architecture that runs Windows and (recently) the Macintosh. Stallman had disdained the Intel architecture because when he started it didn't have the necessary memory protect features; when Torvalds came on the scene, it did.

But the architecture is Stallman's, insofar as Linux differs from the original Unix. Stallman is the true father of Linux.

Except it should be called Gnu/Linux. Some people say "Gnu is a part of Linux." No, Linux is a part of Gnu.

Chapter 11 The World Wars Go Mobile (1983)

> *Summary.* The "desktop computer" is a familiar object descended from the mainframe and Unix concepts of what a computer is. But the same circuits are available now in portable devices, and various schemers are trying to migrate people's work and entertainments from desktop machines into their pockets. Doing quite well, actually—since each transmission costs the consumer money.

Slippery timelines here, but we can say that PDAs and mobile phones began in the early eighties. Both have grown functions in all directions and are trying to compete with desktop machines in organizing people's lives, naturally the way *they* think your lives should be organized.

PDAs. Handheld multipurpose gizmos, or PDAs (Personal Digital Assistants, a term coined by John Sculley) appeared in 1983 with the excellent Psion, in England. (Psion faded into software and became the Symbian operating system, available on a number of Nokia and other phones. But they are being careful not to upset Microsoft.)

The Apple Newton, championed by Sculley, didn't do much. The Palm Pilot series has done much more.

Recently Windows Mobile, upgraded from Windows CE (which was for smallish computers), is capturing a market. However, because the software base underneath is different from standard Windows, developers have to make a big new investment to get on board.

MOBILE PHONES (called **cellphones** in the USA). The mobile phone was patented by Nathan Stubblefield (also the inventor of broadcasting) in 1907. However, it didn't reach the public until the eighties.

Who invented the camera phone? No committees, no market research. Philippe Kahn, wanting to send out pictures of his baby daughter, jury-rigged a camera to his mobile phone; and thus the cameraphone was born. There are now a billion out there.

A NEW WORLD, NOT THE DESKTOP. As digital capabilities get smaller, the PDA and mobile phone can in principle do everything your "computer" (more traditional packaging) can do. How design such a new world? And how sell it, how persuade the public to use it? Rivals are Apple, Google, Microsoft, Blackberry and others.

WINDOWS MOBILE. Microsoft's Windows Mobile is the operating system for a number of mobile phones. (It began as Windows CE for small computers.) One problem for developers is that Windows Mobile does not use the same software libraries as conventional Windows, meaning that development must be separate. This is to the advantage of Microsoft, who want to take care of all your personal information.

THE IPHONE. One man had no difficulty selling a new world around the mobile phone. Steve Jobs decreed the Iphone into existence, oversaw its development, and sold millions in the two years since it exploded onto the market.

ANDROID. Supposedly Google's alternative to the Iphone-- an open source design they've given to the world, called Android-- will give the Iphone a run for its money. But we'll see whether it has the appeal to non-tekkies of the Iphone.

BLACKBERRY. With a solid following, the Blackberry is the addict's email and texting device, but usually on corporate accounts; relatively few are owned by individuals.

JITTERBUG. The expensive "Jitterbug" phone goes the other way. Rather than put applications on it, they are positioned as the Mobile Phone for Seniors-- you pay a lot more for a lot less.

Chapter 12 The Internet-- Enjoy It While You Can (1989)

Summary. The ARPANET disappears in stages, is renamed to "Internet" and opened to the general public. ISPs and long-line providers come into the game.

Now the Internet has become an ocean of communication. By lowering the price of content transfer to nearly zero, the Internet revolutionizes the world. Millions, then billions of users join up. Previously unimaginable opportunities, problems and dangers infest our lives.

All the oldest issues of freedom and tyranny, privacy and speech and press and legal rights of every kind, are thrown onto this stage to fight and fight over. Previously unimagined freedoms and free information abound.

The Internet has no head or center. No one owns it. Its use cannot be controlled. And anyone who sees a new opportunity for mischief or crime can take advantage of it, sending packets to probe, attack and steal.

Governments hate the freedom it gives to citizens. But the Internet may be only our brief moment of freedom, like Periclean Athens; many things may bring it down.

When Did ARPANET become the Internet, open to the public? Not exactly clear; it happened by degrees. Vint Cerf connected MCIMail to the Arpanet (the first consumer service) in 1983. National Science

Foundation (which owned a main trunk) relaxed its rules against commercial development in 1995.

WHO OWNS THE INTERNET? No one. Its parts (the fiber-optic cables and other transmission lines) are owned by different companies and universities The Internet has no head or center. Its use cannot be controlled. Its technical and political aspects are overseen by various committees but they can only recommend--

Overview visualization of part of the Internet, by Matt Britt, from actual data. (Creative Commons Attribution License.)

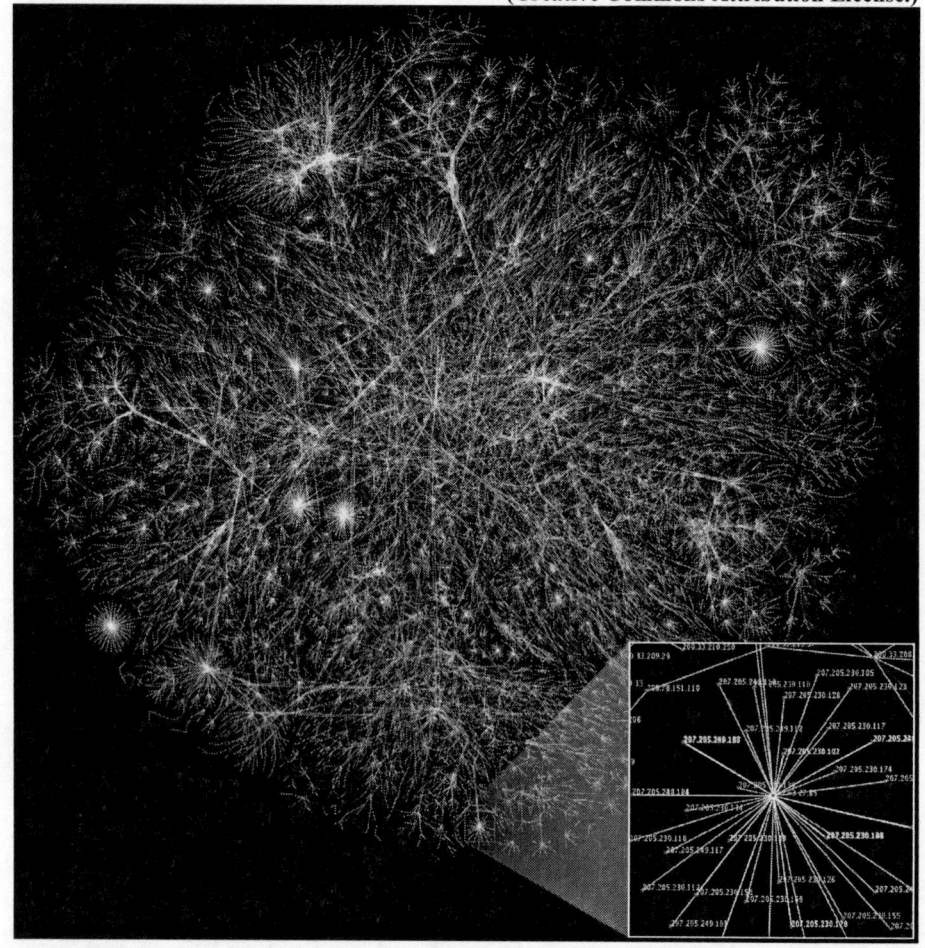

anyone with a server on the Internet can choose to do things differently. And anyone who sees a new opportunity for mischief or crime can take advantage of it, sending packets to probe, attack and steal.

THE DIGITAL DIVIDE. Not only do previously unimaginable opportunities, problems and dangers infest our lives, but many lament the "digital divide" which sets apart those who do not yet have these opportunities, problems and dangers— not quite realizing what they are wishing on the innocent.

All the oldest issues of freedom and tyranny, privacy and speech and press and legal rights of every kind, are thrown onto this stage to fight and fight over. Legal judgments, public debates,

THE FOUR HORSEMEN OF THE INTERNET. No one can argue: we must fight terrorism, child pornography, money laundering and drugs. These are the so-called "four horsemen of the Internet", and tend to put an end to any discussion of freedom or privacy. This is deeply unfortunate, as there are many intermediate issues of great importance.

DISLIKE FROM ABOVE. Many at the top don't like it: governments hate the freedom the Net gives to citizens, and some fear the government will eventually take it away. The Internet may be only our brief moment of freedom, like Periclean Athens; many things may bring it down.

WHAT COULD BREAK THE INTERNET?
- **PHYSICALLY:** Just cutting the main fiber-optic lines, for example. (Such cuts appear to have happened recently as an experiment, possibly by some government.)
- **CLOG.** Once you're connected, there is no marginal cost for Internet usage; you can send (and send for) as much as you like, to (and from) whoever you like, as fast as the messages can go out. This means that trivial downloads (using, say, BitTorrent) have the same priority as government, hospital or bank transactions. In other

words, the bozos can drown the facility. Dealing with this problem is a big controversy among service providers.
- **ROUTER SUBVERSION**. The routers which run the system have back doors for maintenance. Take those over and you can mess up the whole system.
- **IN SOFTWARE**: Distributed denial of service, clogging major servers. Taking down the DNS (which many people say they know how to do). The growing spread of today's zombie botnets (now estimated to include 15% of Windows machines in the world) is creating a force that can be used for great evil. Or just continuing to flood the system with frivolous bandwidth killers, like movies and BitTorrent.
- **POLITICALLY**: Creating some Reichstag Fire/Twin Towers pretext for slamming it shut at the government level. John Walker has written a scary and plausible scenario for this happening: *The Digital Imprimatur: How big brother and big media can put the Internet genie back in the bottle*.§ Larry Lessig, too, has expressed great concerns about the same possibility.

Chapter 13 The Simple Early Web, 1989

Summary. The story in brief: An Oxford-educated idealist at a nuclear research facility creates a system for exchanging writings among physicists, a page distribution scheme with one-way pointers and a simple protocol.

In this system, an ARPANET address can hold a document or a directory. This extends the conventional computer file structure across the world. The curious hybrid structure—hypertext pages and non-page locations-- takes off.

His initial hypertext system is like karaoke-- anyone can do it. Its pages simulate paper; and as with the WYSIWYG documents of the desktop PUI, there is no way to annotate or overlay them.

Talked out of a clumsier name, Berners-Lee says, 'Okay, let's just call it the World Wide Web'. Little does he (or anyone) know.

Tim Berners-Lee, an amiable idealist with a will of iron, moved the hypertext model of HES to network addressing. He bound up one-way links within the file, using the angle-bracket notation of the SGML markup language, and called it HTML, or HyperText Markup Language.

Acknowledging the Xanadu project as one influence, Tim wanted to develop a hypertext system for physics researchers. Looking at the one-way hypertext systems (imitating HES from Brown) and ignoring the two-way link systems of Xanadu and Microcosm, he created a very simple way of delivering one-way hypertext. But to Xanadu alumni it looks illicit and fundamentally broken, making no distinction between a place on the network and a document, and adhering to the old box-of characters model.

Then he created a dirt-simple hypertext system-- the HTTP protocol and the HTML page description language, a secure location for serving pages, and a convention for what page to open first ("index.html").

The page format was based on SGML, a "markup" language which embedded the markup inside the text, following the Seybold/PARC/IBM traditions rather than leaving the text clean and putting the markup on the side.

The great simplicity of doing a few Web pages masks the extraordinary difficulty of maintaining them; the field of Content Management has sprung up to help out. (IBM has nearly given up on maintaining its hundreds of thousands of pages.*)

*IBM insider, personal communication.

But its rough and beguiling simplicity pushes dozens of problems into the laps of users and creates a maintenance nightmare, resulting in the Content Management industry and millions of broken links.

RESULTS OF THE CONSTRUCT:
A strange vocabulary results from this design--
- **website** (cluster of pages arbitrarily connected)
- **home page** (designated starting point for the cluster of pages)
- **webmaster** (a tekkie who has responsibility for the maintenance, appearance and interaction of the cluster of pages-- usually the appearance and interaction get the short end)

Chapter 14 PUI on the Internet-- the Web Browser Salad (1992)

Summary. In a sense the real creators of the Web as we know it are two students at the University of Illinois. Tim Berners-Lee's audaciously-named World Wide Web page distribution system-- files, protocol and one-way connections-- catches the eye of students Marc Andreessen and Eric Bina, who see great possibilities for the Web system and colonize it.

THE FRAMEUP: They design a frame for it, the NCSA Web browser (now just called "the browser"). It is a frame for windowing, decorating and interacting with Web pages. In other words, it is the PARC User Interface (PUI) on the Internet, but with one-way links in addition (as have come down from filesystems and HES).

The browser catches on like wildfire and use grows geometrically. It hits the public in 1994. It starts hosting major commerce around 1996. It reaches a million users, then a billion, and is still growing.

Others rush to put more kinds of interaction into the browser, which becomes Coney Island-- tarted up with JavaScript, Cascading Style Sheets, Flash, Ajax, streaming audio and video. But all of them are locked to a paper-like rectangle. It's still the PARC model of paper under glass, but with interactive acrobatics inside the rectangular page and one-way links between the pages.

The browser defines what is possible on the Web-- and what is impossible.

In a frenetic year, two U. Illinois students—one an undergraduate—managed to maintain a full schedule of courses and yet manage to create a piece of software that changed the world. Working at the National Center for Supercomputer Applications under Larry Smarr, they take the lean, no-system created by Tim Berners-Lee and dress it to the nines, with interactions and gadgets and menus.

The result was the NCSA Browser, trademarked Mosaic.

WHY'D IT CATCH ON? Most important for its catching on, they add pictures. And an easy interface. And formatting. And bookmarks. And cookies. And an editor for simple pages. And the visible URL line. The boys expansively designed a whole way of life, little knowing how many it will ensnare.

In other words, the PARC User Interface (PUI) on the Internet, but with one-way links in addition (as are traditional from the Unix Inode Table).

Andreessen wanted to make the browser a business and was told to seek his fortune elsewhere. He found a backer (Jim Clark, just separated from being CEO of Silicon Graphics) and they founded Silicon Graphics, which went public in the most spectacular offering to that time (some two billion dollars market cap by the end of the day).

Meanwhile, Microsoft licensed the NCSA browser directly from the University of Illinois. Bill Gates saw the World Wide Web and turned Microsoft around in six months. Microsoft gave away their Explorer browser, undercutting Netscape's business, and Netscape barely made it to acquisition by AOL-Time Warner before going bankrupt.

The NCSA browser is now available under many names, including Explorer, Foxfire, Safari, Google Chrome. It defines what is possible on the Web-- and what is impossible, which is anything with visible connection. All you can see is pages, possible jumps, and the URL.

GEEKS BEARING GIFTS

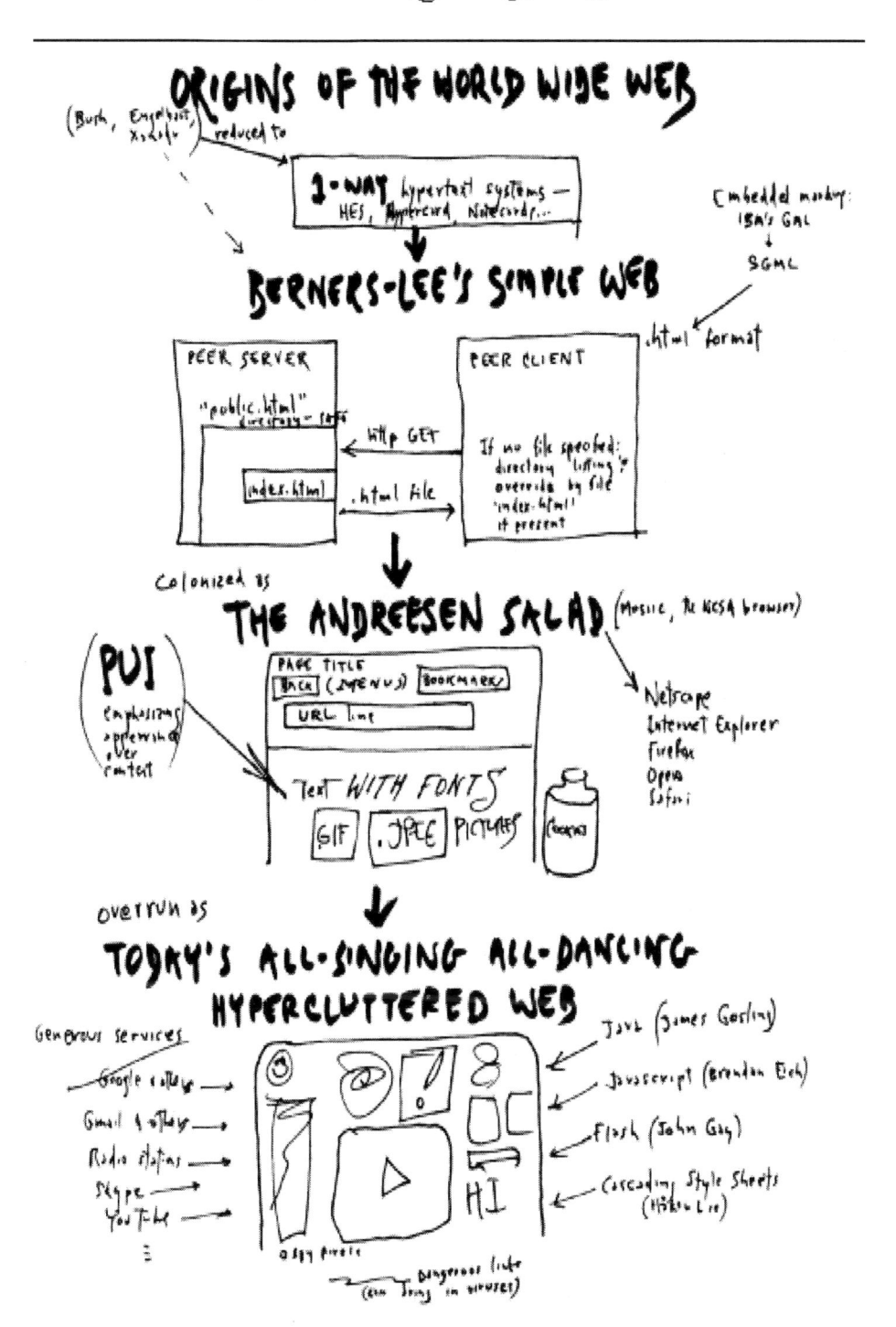

ORIGINS OF THE WORLD WIDE WEB

(Bush, Engelbart, Xanadu) reduced to → 2-WAY hypertext systems — HES, Hypercard, Notecards,...

Embedded markup: IBM's GML → SGML → .html format

BERNERS-LEE'S SIMPLE WEB

PEER SERVER — "public.html" directory — serves
  index.html

← http GET
.html file →

PEER CLIENT
If no file specified: directory listing; overridden by file "index.html" if present

Colonized as ↓

THE ANDREESEN SALAD (Mosaic, the NCSA browser)

PUI
Emphasizing appearance over content

PAGE TITLE
BACK (MENUS) BOOKMARKS
URL line
Text WITH FONTS
GIF .JPEG PICTURES (cookies)

→ Netscape
  Internet Explorer
  Firefox
  Opera
  Safari

overrun as ↓

TODAY'S ALL-SINGING ALL-DANCING HYPERCLUTTERED WEB

Generous services
— Google culture
— Gmail & others
— Radio stations
— Skype
— YouTube
  ⋮

← Java (James Gosling)
← Javascript (Brendan Eich)
← Flash (John Gay)
← Cascading Style Sheets (Håkon Lie)

a spy portal
Dangerous links (can bring in viruses)

Chapter 15 The URL Unifies Net Addresses (1994)

> *Summary.* To fit his World Wide Web distribution scheme, Berners-Lee creates the URL (a uniform way of addressing anything on the Internet).
>
> This makes the network uniformly traversible without special cases, hiding the variety of filesystems. This is a powerful unification of the whole Internet. It can be argued that this is Tim's great contribution to the world, rather than his one-way hypertext system.

(Tim Berners-Lee did not initially release his proposed readdressing method for his World Wide Web scheme, though it was built in from the beginning, so we put it later chronologically.)

To facilitate his hypertext system, Tim created the URL, a uniform way of addressing anything on the Internet. The idea is to reconcile all the different file systems and reference methods and reduce them all to one standard notation. Like the Unix inode table, it makes all resources into one common fabric. (It doesn't force hierarchy because all the systems were hierarchical already.)

This makes the network uniformly traversible without special cases, hiding the variety of filesystem differences, just as TCP/IP hid the varieties of network protocols.

(The URL is actually a special case of the URI, but that explanation is too convoluted even for this volume.)

In a way Tim is like Alcuin the monk (or whoever it was— see Chapter (-26)), when he created for Charlemagne a common Latin writing for all of Europe. The URL integrates the whole net very much the way Medieval Latin united Europe and IP (Internet Protocol) united the

GEEKS BEARING GIFTS   171

ARPANET— hiding the idiosyncrasies of different nodes in a common structure (which, alas, is the hierarchical tradition of the computer field).

That said, the URL is possibly the most user-hostile item that ordinary users ever see; the tangled complexity of that single line in the browser is a model of the difficulties of all the computer world. (Why is a space represented by "%20"? The explanation is too long, but it is a consistent mechanism.)

From left to right the URL contains: protocol, slashes (whose number is important), the top-level domain (confusingly on the right), other chained server directories (on the left with dots, on the right with slashes), file type OR program type (in which case it ends); OR doorway to the database (question mark or colon); then anything beyond the database veil, followed by a file type or program type.

Chapter 16 Web Biz: The Dot-Com World and the New Monopolies (1995)

Summary. Few expect what will happen when business starts up on the Web. From the days of a few professors exchanging files by ARPANET, and the .COM domain (for commerce) an afterthought, few imagined the business expansion of the Internet brought about by the World Wide Web.

Public awareness of the Web begins on a large scale about 1994. Shop windows, secure payment systems began, 'shopping cart' conventions build up, and people begin actually buying things. Smashing old industries on every side, threatening every form of commerce and business and providing startling new opportunities, the new way of doing business confuse everyone into a variety of sometimes-idiotic strategies. To do nothing seems worse than doing something, anything.

The bubble bursts in 2000 with the dot-com crash.

The world picks itself up again and now the dot-com cycle is repeating.

Meanwhile, the old order changeth: big old companies lie by the wayside, and we see the new monopolies-- Adobe, Amazon, Ebay (which began by auctioning a broken laserpointer), PayPal, Wikipedia, CraigsList, BitTorrent, Google, YouTube, Lulu.com. These companies are like nothing that ever happened before, each with its own odd story.

Following Netscape's unprecedented two-billion-dollar stock sale, the new "dot-com" companies proliferated, seeking ever-more-idiotic names that would be unique on the net. Going public with no revenues and trying to get big fast was not a sustainable business model. The bubble burst in 2000, with the Dot-Com Crash.

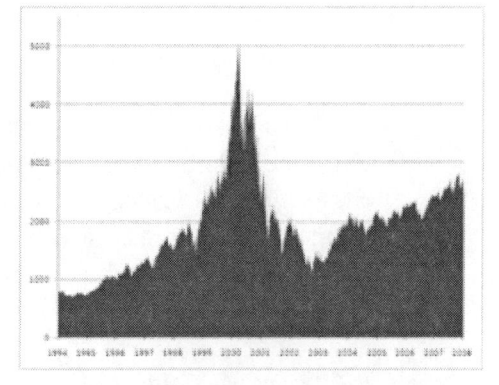

NASDAQ prices, the best indicator of speculative investment, 2994-present. The Dot-com peak is clearly visible. Source: "The Little Professor", Kazakhstan.

In the ensuing ecology of business on the net, new companies have replaced old ones in remarkable ways.

Big old companies have lost big. They thought they could move into the new-- but not with their old attitudes. The giants fell one by one-- Xerox, IBM, AOL, Britannica, Barnes (& Noble), Compu-Serve (so recently on top of networking), AOL Time-Warner (so recently on top of networking).

NEW GIANTS. Instead now we have the new giants--

> **AMAZON** (founded by sparkplug Jeff Bizos) is the most like a conventional company of old— it's a big old mail-order house, but with pazazz. It's lost some of the original spice, though: in the good old days of Amazon, they actually had a a click-box by a book saying "I AM THE AUTHOR OF THIS BOOK," then allowed you to make corrections or reply. No more.
>
> **EBAY** is unlike anything anyone's seen. It began when the founder Pierre Omidyar auctioned a broken laserpointer on the net and got more than the new price. Astutely staying out of guaranteeing anything, Ebay instead creates a Reputation System

that shames bad players—supposedly. Unfortunately Ebay is now being gamed in complex ways that make it harder to use—programmed bidding down to the wire, for example.

YOUTUBE. Three young guys working at PayPal (Chad Hurley, Steve Chen and Jawed Karim) came up with an audacious idea. Betting that the advertising revenue would outstrip the cost of storing vast amounts of video and their socket connections, two upstart kids created a huge repository for user-supplied videos. It worked and Google bought it for $1.65 billion.

CISCO. Cisco, the router kings, rule the Internet, although there are smaller startups like Barracuda. Founded by Len Bosack and Sandy Lerner, a married couple who worked in computer ops at Stanford, Cisco started making multi-protocol routers and now has 66,000 employees.

GOOGLE. See Chapter 18.

WIKIPEDIA. See Chapter 20.

FREEBIE-RAMA. In the new dot-com bubble, companies have found it pays to give away vast resources to customers (mainly disk space)-- Hotmail, Yahoo Mail, Gmail, Skype, YouTube, backup services-- in hopes of some users paying for more.

> [Note: if you want to sign up for some free account on the Web, but not be stuck on their mailing list, go to bugmenot.com. They'll give you an email address and password for that particular service provider that will satisfy that provider and keep them out of your hair.]

Now people are expecting everything to be free. But let us be mindful of Damon Knight's "To Serve Man"-- the story of a race of superbeings who give mankind everything, based on a manual called *To Serve Man*. It turns out this is a cookbook.

Chapter 17 Streaming Goes Private (1995)

Summary. Streaming is not magic. Audio and video slide across the net using the same techniques of transmission as in email and file transfer, differently treated. (Streaming is considered part of "the Web" now because it uses Web pages as portals, though the protocols are as different from the Web as email.)

Based on the Unix and Internet cooperative spirit, there used to be a great dream of standard formats for streaming audio and video, including VOIP, Voice Over Internet Protocol.

But now all of that is swept away: the open standards are diminishing to niche status, pushed aside by private methods, and monopolies have moved in. What we see now are mostly the special methods of RealNetworks, Apple QuickTime, Skype and YouTube.

BROADCASTING. Broadcasting was first demonstrated by Nathan Stubblefield in 1902 (with electrical waves through the ground). Radio broadcasting began in 1906; advertising came soon after. Government authorization of frequencies, officially intended to prevent signal interference, also helped censorship and strengthened station monopolies.

Scheduled radio broadcasting began in Argentina in 1920. Television broadcasting officially began in 1937, but with methods that were superseded when television began in earnest after the war.
Now the Internet offers a strange new form of broadcasting, where each user has his own streaming channel—in principle changeable depending on whatever factors the broadcasters care about.

It is the same technique(s) of transmission as in email and file transfer, applied to blocks of audio and video; except with different priorities. With email, the important thing is for everything to get through; with streaming, the important thing is to keep up the pace, and fill in the gaps in audio and video as best possible. For instance, if the transmission rate drops, let the video freeze and keep the audio going smoothly; this is the prefereable user experience.

But the fundamental problem is that a stream on the Net is not sent out in one direction but needs 2-way push-pull; because of TCP/IP, there must be an active socket on the server for each recipient. This puts a tremendous load on the servers.

(In the early Internet days there was an "Mbone", a distribution system for many users, to lighten this burden for the streaming party-- but it had to be scheduled, like a radio station).

THE BABEL. It's a Babel now, with a great variety of formats. You can get several channels at once.

Realnetworks (with RealAudio) got an early lead for on-line radio. Apple has also moved in, assimilating their streaming to Quicktime, Apple's media wrapper.

Three different audio streams clog the bandwidth on one user's machine.

Streaming in mp3 followed (a more open standard, used by such on-line stations as kcrw.com), but Realnetworks kept upgrading and offering more.

Skype has left behind public standards to offer private service-- the first part of which is free.

VIDEO: Apple introduced QuickTime, which was a wrapper for video and audio as well, presenting either content local on your machine or streamed on the net.

Flash has its own streaming methods.

YouTube, offering users free video storage and presentation, uses a Flash client and lo-res video.

Now even the BBC, if you want to hear it on line, gives you a choice of only Realnetworks and Windows Media. And kcrw.com has dropped mp3 for only proprietary formats.

Chapter 18 Google (1996)

Summary. Two clever and careful Stanford students take over the world one step at a time, but moving audaciously from the beginning. First with a super search engine. Then they figure out how to make money, getting the trick from another company. Then they go public their own way (kind of), for apocalyptic profit.

Google now has the largest computer-- i.e., unified computer system-- in the world (thought to be well over a million processors), with the most reliable operating system in the world-- a distributed parallel Gnu/Linux that never stops, even as disk drives die constantly. (Hey, if something's missing, how would you know?)

ORGANIZATION. Google is a very flat company (no new project is vital). It's very tough to get hired, requiring many interviews. Employees make bargains with their bosses on their proposed projects, and then better deliver. The company is tightly run by two software veterans, Eric Schmidt and Peter Norvig; as well as by the founders (who also get to jet around and hold pep rallies for the employees).

Google threatens every content industry, publishing industry and library industry. "This is a wake-up call," says an executive at the Bibliothèque national de France. "We thought we could take much longer to get around to it."

Sergei Brin and Larry Page probably did not expect all this, but Oh Well. First came their new Web search engine. The immensity of their plan-- to cache and maintain a copy of the entire Web-- was monumental. But they saw the falling prices of disk drives and they knew how to use Unix very well. They customized Gnu/Linux for parallel operation their own way (since they aren't giving it away, they don't have to make the enhancements public).

The success of their company, Google, has been monumental. It is presently worth 186 billion dollars (market cap)—among the top American corporations.

HOW IT WORKS. Their trick is to rank listings by how many other links point to them. But it's not as simple as that. Their famous page rank algorithm is a closely-guarded secret (so publicists can't game it), but the components aren't that complicated. What the page-rank discussion does is distract from how they do it:

They dared to cache every page and index every word in sorting grids. A three-word inquiry jumps to a listing for the first word, then jumps to a listing for the first and second word, then to a listing for all three words, then gave you the list of pages. (A simple Google query may go through 900 processors in the network, says the S.F. Chronicle (mid-2008).)

In 2006 the Google system was estimated to be 250,000 computers. Now it's surely over a million, and they're talking ten million at a thousand locations (don't know where, do you? They like it that way).

Much of the Google code is in Python.

¿**HOW COME?** How'd the boys get the project away from Stanford, a notoriously grabby university? The story will be clarified over the years. Certainly when they went public they gave stock to the board of directors (as individuals), but that was late in the game.

THIS JUST IN: Google has concluded a lawsuit with the U.S. publishing industry and acquired the right to serve snippets of content from present books, as well as all the books they have scanned. Google now owns all of literature.

Chapter 19 Cyberfashion (1996)

Summary. The founding moment of the Internet social elite comes in 1996, when John Perry Barlow's ringing declaration demands that network users be exempted from all terrestrial laws. His eloquent if baffling challenge is some kind of classic.

The fashion center of today's computer world is Wired magazine, a garish monthly designed to make readers feel they're at the center of digital action. Like Apple's products, Wired is as much a fashion statement as a substantive product, to be worn by those who want to be With It.

John Brockman, a literary agent, defines the cyberfashion food chain. Brockman tells book publishers who and what matters. The last decade's computer trade books bear the Brockman imprint.

Internet fashion statements are being made worldwide. The most charming is the Chinese couple who try to name their child "@".

Under every new regime there is a new social and fashion elite. Besides the everyday work and craziness of the Internet, there are those with special claims to attention in this new world.

THAT JUNK-WORD, CYBER-. Most terms beginning with "cyber-" are inane; the term can best be translated as "I don't know what I'm talking about." Notable, however, is Norbert Wiener's defining book *Cybernetics* (1948), where he actually meant *control linkages*. But that core meaning got way lost in the shuffle.

THE BARLOW DECREE. The founding manifesto of this world might be taken as John Perry Barlow's ringing 1996 "A Declaration of the Independence of Cyberspace"§, a sort of "Rights of Man" transposed to the New Order. He declared freedom and independence for all the netizens of cyberspace, meaning ARPANET users. Asserting that this group constituted a new country with new prerogatives and no location, Barlow demanded exemption for on-line users from all laws of earthly nations. His eloquent plea made it into a lot of textbooks, but no one in the political or judicial world even scratched their heads.

WIRED. Fashion center of today's computer world is Wired magazine, a garish monthly designed to make readers feel they're at the center of the action. Like Apple's products, Wired is as much a fashion statement as a substantive product, to be worn by those who want to be With It.

Like any magazine, Wired's principal concern is of course to sell advertising, and more even than most magazines they have to keep up a drumfire of novelty, to make you feel that you can't keep up with this new world without them. But the Wired party line is specific in a number of directions. As the principal celebrants and sycophants of the World Wide Web, they have been known to launch savage personal attacks on those who criticize the Web's premises.

Louis Rossetto, founder of Wired, now has a chocolate company. It is to be hoped that his chocolate is less poisonous than his journalism.

THE BROCKMAN STABLE. John Brockman, a literary agent, is the shadowy figure at the top of the cyberfashion food chain. Arranging publishers for such Wired authors as Howard Rheingold, Kevin Kelly and Stewart Brand, Brockman tells the slightly clueless book publishers who and what matters. Many of the current decade's books bear the Brockman viewpoint, which is close to that of Wired. Dissenting points of view will not appear through the Wired or Brockman pipelines.

A CHILD NAMED @. Internet fashion statements are being made worldwide. The most charming is the Chinese couple who recently tried to name their child "@". Yes, @ is now a legitimate character in Unicode, and it has a nice punful pronunciation in Mandarin Chinese. But what would be the child's email address? It would probably be blocked somewhere along the line.

Chapter 20 Web 2.0-- Community and Cattle Pen

> *Summary.* "Web 2.0" and "social media" are journalists' phrases to lump together a bunch of stuff on the Net, made to seem oh so new. They generally refer to Facebook, MySpace, Second Life and Wikipedia (and ever so many other wannabes). These services, like so many others on the net, are contrived to capture customers.

"COMMUNITY". Everyone says they want 'community' on the Internet. But what can that possibly mean? You may exchange messages with them, but the hard fact is: these are people you can't see, who may be fooling you (possibly with elaborate software ruses for theft), and may not even exist.

But what's so new about social media? Email was always a social medium! Facebook, Myspace and their imitators are essentially the same internal techniques as email and the Web, just different packaging.

WIKIPEDIA, "articles you can edit yourself". Everyone agrees that Wikipedia is great; Richard Dawkins has called it "a miracle".

Journalists lump Wikipedia with Facebook and MySpace but it's quite different. But it's not what it claims to be. Yes anyone can edit it, temporarily, but not really. Your "edit" might just as well be put in a submission window, because it will be scrutinized and judged by the REAL editors.

> Attention: As of 2007-05-22, I have ceased editing Wikipedia indefinitely. I can no longer deal with the broken and counterproductive prevailing interpretations and applications of well-intended policies, the total lack of initiative to make tough decisions needed to keep things on track, the sheer impossibility of finding consensus in highly polarized debates, and especially the politics. This page is preserved a— **Wikipedia, "User:Matt Britt"** §
>
> Resignation note of Matt Britt, high-level Wikipedia editor.

And Wikipedia is very political. Wikipedia runs on volunteer labor, lots of it. The internal politics are fierce. The guys behind the scenes have the last word. Those real editors are guys who work their way up through the subculture (like anywhere else). Indeed, Wikipedia can be considered to be a Massive Multiplayer Role-Playing Game (see Chapter (-14)) where the Quests are not about dragons and chests of loot but about what viewpoint a big article is going to have.

Wikipedia is a fake in one conspicuous respect: when you "edit" an article, it is actually a submission that may stand briefly, but will be considered by the *real* editors.

It's not generally known that Wikipedia is built on a key part of the Xanadu data structure; each page is a series of quotations, or transclusions, from separate editing operations.   See article "Wikipedia:Transclusion" at Wikipedia (no spaces).§

ORIGIN OF WIKIPEDIA. It is sometimes alleged that Wikipedia founder Jimmy "Jimbo" Wales was a pornographer. This is an exaggeration. (His stuff was soft-core.) He began by setting up an encyclopedia with thoroughly-reviewed articles, and after a year there were only a couple. Then he set it up as a wiki, or everybody-editable system, and it took off. But the organizational problems behind the scenes are enormous and probably permanent. "Don't expect articles to get better," says a long-time Wikipedia watcher.

THE BIG SOCIAL SITES

Friendster, Facebook, MySpace and imitators are ways that people can present themselves without having to create whole Web pages, and ways they can communicate with friends, make more. To those who like them they are very involving.

> **Friendster** was founded by Jonathan Abrams in 2002, and was thought of as a way of safely making new friends.
>
> **Facebook** was founded by Harvard sophomore Mark Zuckerberg in 2004. First limited to Harvard students, it recruited half of them

within a month. It then opened to other Ivy League schools, then the world. Now it's quite big.

MySpace. MySpace was founded out of Friendster and Euniverse by people we won't try to list. It's now owned by Rupert Murdoch (Fox Interactive, Beverly Hills). Your page can be more decorated than in Facebook.

Second Life. Philip Rosedale, a physics major from U.Cal San Diego, founded Linden Lab in 1999 to build hot 3D hardware. But he saw that people were more interested in what you could DO in these spaces, so Second Life was born.

Second Life takes place on an archipelago of 3D islands hosted on computers in San Francisco. You fire up their client software-- they require hot machines-- and now can fly around their 3D world. You have to choose a first and last name; they offer a limited supply of last names but more choice for the first. You can choose how you look. You can fly around and go to all sorts of places.

Here's the kicker: you can rent a space, or a whole island, for real money. You can create 3D objects using their programming system, and sell those 3D objects for real money. Linden Labs always gets a cut.

There are many places and activities to see, some Naughty; you can attend meetings, walk down streets, even fly. Indeed, Second Life can be deeply absorbing, or the Ultimate Time-Waster. It has been alleged that women like Second Life more than men: 'It's dolls' houses.' But these figures are not available.

CONSTRUCT PACKAGES. Essentially these are construct packages that put together the same innards as other software, but create artificial places and set up carefully-structured ways to communicate with those you know and those you don't. The thing to remember, however, is that it's all about keeping you involved and exposing you to ads.

Specific arrangements require your attention all the time. If you join Facebook, for example, you are constantly pestered by people who say they want to be your friend; now you must decide whether they are (a chance to pester you further) or not (in which case their feelings will be hurt).

So this is not "technology". It is a system of constructs about social life, but formalizing it in new ways, that enmesh people and keep them busy. Some would say cattle pens.

REAL COLLABORATION ON THE NET: Bob Carlson's achievement at Citibank. Bob Carlson was just your average vice president of Citibank when the word came from above: all the computer operations of Citibank would have to be consolidated and unified.

Carlson spoke up and gave several reasons why this was absolutely impossible.

All who heard greatly appreciated his understanding of the problem. And so he was told: *"Good, you're in charge."*

It took a couple of years. He set up world-wide teams to select the problems and work them out, including an überteam to decide what teams were needed. *No managers were allowed on the teams.* The whole thing was done without managers, except Bob, who took a facilitative role and let the teams make every decision. It all worked.*
Bob is now at the redoubtable Oxford Internet Institute.

*Bob Carlson, personal communication.

The problem seems to be that to use this method, you have to be Bob Carlson. He should write a book. Or get his teams to write it.

Chapter 21 The Myth of Computer Technology

> ***Summary.*** Much of what is called "computer technology" consists of conventions, packages, constructs arbitrarily designed. These were chosen by various individuals, projects, companies, marketing campaigns and accidents. And there are always fights and controversies.
>
> "Technology" is simply the chessboard on which these other games are played.

You've been taught that Computer Technology is inexorable, inevitable, and required. The way things are is how they have to be, it's all necessary and good-- WYSIWHAM, What You See Is Wonderfully, Happily, Absolutely Mandatory.

Perhaps this book has helped you understand that this attitude is bunk. Thousands of decisions and fights, in many companies and attics, have led to the present situation; it could have come out many different ways, and still might.

The myth of computer technology is that it has some compelling necessity of its own, forcing itself on us.

This myth of technological necessity has stifled people's imaginations. And their willingness to demand more and better.

CONSTRUCTS

Almost everything you see on your computer screen is a *construct*— something people have imagined to present to you. Constructs are not technology in themselves.

The constructs of hierarchical directories in the 1950s, the constructs of the PARC group in 1974 were chosen for you because they were simple.

Today's constructs are more convoluted, but they are still imaginary concepts somebody built--
    Word processors,
    Email,
    windows (generic),
    Windows (Microsoft),
    IMAGINARY SPACES-- Facebook, movie editing systems, playlists, chat rooms, social spaces (or dungeons) of many chambers to hold users.

These are all constructs, not technology. Somebody made them up. Yes, there is Technology underneath, but the idea generally comes first, and then people figure out mechanisms to make it work.

(Although often people's preferred technical methods get into the act and strongly affect the way the ideas come out; but we won't get into that here.)

PACKAGES. Packages grow out of constructs: when there are constructs, people package them up. For instance, once there was the construct of an email message, Larry Roberts created a package to read a number of them at a time. Thus began the package called the email client. (Today's packages have gotten bigger and bigger.)

CONVENTIONS. Constructs become conventions as people get used to them. Note the received iron conventions of the computer world—
- hierarchical files (from the 1950s)
- document as a long string or lump box of text characters (1960s?)

- the PUI, hardly changed at all since PARC (1974) and Macintosh (1984). The conventions are frozen, with no innovations. For instance, nearly every "clipboard" implemented in the world still holds only one item.

These are all constructs of the mind; the technology is just support.

CAPTURE. Much software is about user capture.

In the ideal world of open source and reusable software objects, users might flit about like butterflies in a garden, using parts from here and there however they would.

In the real world, however, software manufacturers want to capture you as a user and have you never leave. This means addicting you to habits of work, menus, work environment. It means data capture in formats that you can't get out of— or that lose some of their properties, like Microsoft Word documents, when the contents are copied out or converted. It can also mean buying up the competition and making it disappear, to keep people stuck in your system.

That's always been how business works. Consider the Einstein-Szilard refrigerator. It's not generally known that Einstein and Szilard invented and patented a refrigerator with no moving parts; but the patent was bought up by a big appliance company to keep it off the market and hang onto their captive user base. (Einstein and Szilard's later proposal, for a nuclear bomb, was much more influential.) One of these days somebody is going to actually start manufacturing the Einstein fridge.

COMPETING IDEAS. In the world of "technology", ideas have always competed. Important examples are the width of railroad tracks and the issue of space colonization.

Brunel versus the Carriage-Makers. In the early 19th Century, when railroading began, there were two competing widths of railroad track. One of the greatest engineers of all time, Isembard Kingdom Brunel, insisted that the tracks should be wide, for speed and safety. He was right. However, the other makers of train cars insisted that track separation should be a narrower and more traditional width, rumored to have come down from the Roman chariot. Who won? The traditionalists with the chariot width, because of a large installed base.

von Braun versus Lyndon Johnson. The early American space program, in the 1950s and 1960s, was run by Werner von Braun, forgiven for his part in Nazi rocketry. There is some indication that von Braun wanted to colonize space. (This was also the dream of a generation of science-fiction fans who grew up in the 1950s reading Robert Heinlein, who propagandized for colonizing space by private enterprise.) But Lyndon Johnson got funding for NASA essentially as a pork-barrel gift to his home state of Texas, and NASA became staffed by bureaucrats with no interest in space colonization, only in their jobs and suburban lives. The result: today's public apathy about NASA and space doings. However, now that NASA is out of money, private rocketry is now authorized, and privatized space colonies may happen.

These examples show the kinds of fights and policy issues that pervade all of "technology". There are always alternatives with consequences. People care about the different possible outcomes. And there is rarely any determinate right answer based on technical considerations.

So don't fall for the word "technology". It's intended to make you submissive.

Chapter 22 Why We Fight

> In his classic WWII film series, "Why We Fight", Capra explained to U.S. troops that their adversaries were not bad people but misguided. In this book I have striven to express the same respect for those with whom I disagree, and their achievements, even if I consider them wrongful.

Summary. Today's computer world is a godawful mess, ghastly for many people. But there may yet be hope.

I see today's computer world as a nightmare honkytonk prison, noisy and colorful and wholly misbegotten. We are imprisoned in applications that can be customized only in ways the designers allow. We are in a Dark Age of documents, locked in imprisoning formats, canopic jars from which they can never escape, or mangled within by markup which hinders re-use, indexing, connection and overlay and overlap. A blighted parody of the computer dreams we had long ago, it's like being stuck in a fast-food restaurant with all its posters, toys and mess, and pretending we're in paradise.

Many people shrug off the issues discussed here. To me they are some of the most important issues of civilization, buried too long and miscelebrated in the wrong directions.

Much of today's software (particularly the infrastructure you don't see) is wonderful. But much of what you see is bloated and imprisoning.

GEEKS BEARING GIFTS

Some are joyously happy with the way things are. Some feel oppressed, confused, resentful. Both are right: everyone should have the software and interfaces they want. But this is still far from possible. (The Unix ideal of decades ago has not made it into the consumer market.)

We need software where things can criss-cross and overlap and interpenetrate like the real concerns of our documents and lives, and like (for instance) the topics of this book. If your work is a unified conglomerate that does not divide the way the software does, if your life is a unified conglomerate that you wish to manage from computers that are set up all wrong, you see the problem.

Not everyone does.

Today's computer world is perhaps best symbolized by the logo of ClarisWorks 95— three gears which cannot possibly turn.

But software development is not easy, and innovation is tough and political. Stallman did it the right way, not having to argue with anybody. Media innovation, which I and others have attempted, is a dangerous occupation. Gutenberg went bankrupt. Stubblefield, inventor of broadcasting and the mobile phone, supposedly starved to death and was eaten by rats.*

*We are still trying to track this down.

Let us be optimistic. Who knows what may yet be possible? All the ideas have not yet been tried.

And what would you want now if there were a real choice?

Think about it.

TN

=30=•